Quantum Skills for Coaches: A Handbook for Working with
Energy and the Body-Mind in Coaching

© 2008 Annette Simmons

ISBN: 978–1–906316–17–4

Published by Word4Word, Evesham, UK
www.w4wdp.com

The right of Annette Simmons to be identified
as the author of this work has been asserted by
her in accordance with the Copyright, Designs
& Patents Act 1988.

A CIP record of this book is available from the
British Library.

Printed in the UK by TJ International Ltd, Padstow, Cornwall.

CONTENTS

Thank you viii

Foreword ix

PART ONE
What are the Quantum Skills for Coaches?

CHAPTER ONE: What has 'quantum' got to do with it? 3

What does quantum theory say? 6

The energy of thoughts 9

CHAPTER TWO: Where do the quantum skills for coaches come from? 13

My 'well of pain' experience 15

Being 'in the present moment' 18

Focusing 20

Quantum physics 20

Reiki 25

Creative visualisation 27

Psychodrama 28

Cognitive behaviour therapy 29

CHAPTER THREE: Aren't you breaking the 'rules of coaching'? 33

Are we stepping over the coaching boundary and into therapy? 34

Are coaches supposed to give advice? 40

PART TWO
The Tool Kit

Introduction 46

CHAPTER FOUR: Tool One: visualisation – everything is connected 49

Energy goes where attention flows 53

Presenting this tool to your clients 56

CHAPTER FIVE: Our emotions 59

What is an emotion? 60

The reason for having emotions 61

Tool Two: the awareness muscle 62

Fast and slow feelings 66

CHAPTER SIX: Working with our emotions 69

The limbic brain 70

Mirror neurons 71

Serotonin 73

Synchrony and serotonin 74

CHAPTER SEVEN: Choice is the most powerful tool we have 77

Tool Three: E+R=O 78

CHAPTER EIGHT: Managing our emotions 87

Gaining control over your physiology 88

Tool Four: deep breathing 88

Tool Five: focusing. 92

Terry's magic headache cure 97

PART THREE
Working with the Tool Kit

CHAPTER NINE: Energy in our bodies. 103

The body-mind 104

Everything is a hologram 105

Using the focusing technique to explore an issue 107

Case Study One. 107

Piles of sand. 110

Analysis of the case study 112

Integration 116

Applied kinesiology. 117

CHAPTER TEN: The energy in words. 121

Affirmations 123

Contra-indications and negative scripting. 125

**CHAPTER ELEVEN: Awareness of the energy of words in
offering feedback** 129

Why offer feedback?. 130

How to offer feedback 131

The rules of giving feedback. 132

Offering feedback on the words the client uses 138

CHAPTER TWELVE: Offering feedback about other observations. 143

The smile survey. 147

More on feedback 149

Case Study Two. 150

Feedback as a pointer to an underlying issue. 151

Case Study Three. 152

Analysis of the case study 155

CHAPTER THIRTEEN: Feedback about the impact of the client's behaviour upon you 159

Case Study Four 161

When not to give feedback or coaching. 164

CHAPTER FOURTEEN: How coaching outcomes are affected by the coach's beliefs 167

CHAPTER FIFTEEN: Intuition 173

Case Study Five. 176

Analysis of the case study 179

The feeling-being. 184

CHAPTER SIXTEEN: The power of metaphor and the now . . 189

The power of the present moment 191

CHAPTER SEVENTEEN: Power and confidence. 193

How we give away our power. 197

Case Study Six 199

Case Study Seven 201

Analysis of Case Study Six and Case Study Seven. 207

Keystone beliefs a coach must hold 209

When the client cannot recall past confidence 211

CHAPTER EIGHTEEN: Problem solving and creative thinking 215

The problem-solving mindset 216

Appreciative enquiry 218

Brainstorming 220

Case Study Eight 221

Reverse brainstorming 222

CHAPTER NINETEEN: Psychodrama 225

Case Study Nine 226

CHAPTER TWENTY: Universal laws 229

Law of Potentiality. 231

Law of Cause and Effect, or Karma 232

(Law of) Being in the Present. 232

Law of Detachment 232

Case Study Ten 233

Develop an attitude of gratitude. 236

Further reading 237

Index 241

Thank you

My deepest thanks go firstly to all the clients and colleagues who suggested that I write this book and to those clients who allowed me to tell their stories in the case studies.

Thank you also to my dearest husband Terry for your unfailing love and support while these quantum skills found their way into my coaching practice. Without the encouragement and enthusiasm of my three wonderful children and many dear friends and clients who believed in this amazing process, I might have just happily continued to bumble along practising quantum skills rather than sharing them with others. The list with all of your names would be long indeed, but each of you knows who you are – so, thank you. And to my publisher for believing in me at the end of the process – thank you!

Foreword

As a doctor specialising in mind-body medicine and founder of The Academy of Human Potential I am delighted to have been invited to write a Foreword to Annette's book. I regard her approach to coaching not as a replacement to traditional coaching methods but as an enhancement.

The philosophy behind standard coaching is that the client knows the solutions to his issues and challenges but doesn't know that he knows them. The role of the coach is to ask questions to help the client explore his issues from a different perspective and to reveal these solutions which are obscured by the limiting beliefs which distort reality and confuse the mind. Quantum skills for coaches takes this philosophy to another dimension and rather than ask questions of the client's 'mind which-is-in-his-brain' the coach asks questions of the client's 'mind-which-is-in-his-body'. The body-mind is not subject to the distortions of the client's limiting beliefs but speaks its truth from its position in the present moment. The straightforward (though usually metaphorical) story which unfolds as the body literally *speaks its mind* in this way, is a very different one from the often plaintive, victim-tinged tale of woe narrated by the brain and it leads to a clarity of perception and understanding that is astounding in both its immediacy and swiftness.

This book is an important contribution to the development and evolution of the field of coaching and I invite you to try out her tools for yourself, and for your clients, because they really do work.

Dr Mark Atkinson, author of *The Mind-Body Bible* and *Holistic Health Secrets for Women*, and Founder of The Academy of Human Potential.
www.drmarkatkinson.com

PART ONE

What are the Quantum Skills for Coaches?

CHAPTER ONE

What has 'quantum' got to do with it?

Once upon a time a child was born. She was like a castle – a magnificent castle with many spacious, sumptuously furnished rooms which she was free to roam, explore and enjoy to her heart's content.

Then, one day, when the child laughed in delight because she misunderstood that something serious was happening, the horrified grown-ups exclaimed "How could you laugh at something like that? What a rude child you are!" and the door of one of the rooms slammed shut.

From then onwards, each time someone said to her "How dare you", "Don't be like that", "How disgusting!", "Look what she just did!", "That's not nice", "People like us don't do that!", another door slammed tightly shut. Gradually there were fewer and fewer rooms for the child to visit and, after a while, she forgot that she ever was a castle. Over the years, the child diminished so much that eventually she came to see herself as no more than a shabby two-bedroomed semi in dire need of repair.

This child is all of us.

This book is written so that you, as a coach, can help your clients to reach deep inside themselves, find the keys that will unlock the doors and step once again into each forgotten room. You will watch with joy as your clients fling open the windows to streams of sunlight, learn to reinhabit and enjoy these spaces and reclaim the far-reaching views from the windows, which are their birthright.

It will also help you to rediscover your own forgotten rooms.

I am assuming that, if you are reading this book, you are working as a coach and may hold a coaching qualification or two. You may be working in the corporate field or as a life coach. Or you may be one of the many specialist coaches who focus on a single aspect of a client's life or experience (such as relationships, parenting, weight loss or quitting smoking) or perhaps you coach engineers, advertising executives or accountants because of your specific experience in that field. Maybe you are not a coach but are thinking of becoming one or are currently being coached and want to understand more about the process. If you fall into either of the latter two categories, you may not find this book as helpful as a more general book to introduce you to coaching techniques. I am writing principally for a reader who already has a firm, basic understanding of the coaching process, tools and techniques, which enables me to refer to these without describing them in detail.

So, what are the quantum skills for coaches and how will they open these doors? They describe the place where quantum physics meets 'the human condition' and it describes an approach to coaching that will broaden the scope of your current skills. They will also take you on an adventure that will expand your understanding of how our internal processes operate and reveal a new dimension of the possibilities that, as human beings, we all hold within us. Possibilities for stepping into our full power and becoming the finest version of ourselves that we can possibly be. Possibilities for doing whatever it is that we are here to do.

We hear the word 'quantum' all around us today – quantum theory, quantum healing, quantum cookery, quantum this that and the other. 'Quantum leap', though, has been part of our vocabulary for some years, and the link between this kind of momentous change and quantum skills is significant. To take a quantum leap also suggests a fearless and intuitive leap of faith. Being coached in this way is certainly a quantum leap into the unfamiliar for clients as well as for coaches who learn to put their trust in this amazing process.

So then, what is the relationship between quantum physics and the human condition? According to the dictionary, quantum theory is:

> *"a theory describing the behaviour and interactions of elementary particles or energy states based on the*

assumptions that energy is subdivided into discrete amounts and that matter possesses wave properties".

This sounds like a 'hard-to-get-your-brain-around' conversation-stopper for eggheads. Not at all! I failed physics at school rather spectacularly many years ago but am, nevertheless, totally fascinated by what this theory says and its implications for our lives – so I can assure you that you don't need a rigorous scientific mindset to appreciate it. In the same way that we are able to drive a car without a full understanding of mechanics, or appreciate music on CD without learning about the recording process, we can grasp what quantum theory tells us about our world without being able to decipher the scientific formulae that prove it.

However, if you do want to read more about the science than I will cover here, there are numerous books and other sources that might interest you. Try, for example, *The Self Aware Universe* and *The Quantum Doctor* by quantum physicist Amit Goswami, and the many books and articles quoted on http://en.wikipedia.org/wiki/Quantum_mechanics

What does quantum theory say?

Quantum theory puts forward many fascinating concepts, which, when applied to our experiences, can offer profound insights into the way we create and respond to life's circumstances. Therefore, since coaching is a tool for helping us to create and respond to our life's events in ways that are helpful to us rather than hold us back, 'quantum' is a word that can have a great relevance to coaching. I would add here that the beliefs I hold about the connection between quantum theory and the way we live our lives may seem rather unusual, and if you are of an analytical nature you may wonder about the logic in my leaps of reasoning. I would simply ask you to bear with me as I work through it, and the logic will emerge.

Now, I am not about to describe all there is to know about quantum physics – this would be a challenging task indeed. It is a huge and complex field of which I have only a comparative wisp of an understanding, especially given my track record in physics studies! Instead, I will walk you through those aspects that have grabbed my attention because of their pragmatic application to the human condition and their link back to ancient wisdom which describes the universal laws governing our experiences and, strangely enough, say very similar things to quantum physics. If you were to read an article by any modern-day quantum physicist about, say, the nature of matter, and compare it with a piece of writing by any one of the ancient mystics about the same thing, you would find that it is impossible to tell one from the other. They would both use the same kind of language to describe this concept, and might contain phrases like "the suchness is curved . . .", because there is no everyday way to describe these concepts that are such a challenge to our day-to-day thinking.[1] Nevertheless, once the physicists have decided what words to use to describe their findings, they can then translate them into more understandable explanations, and I will attempt to convey some of these to you. In this chapter, I will cover just a couple of the aspects of quantum theory that caught my attention and others I will introduce later on.

One of the significant statements that quantum theory makes is that everything that exists is made up of tiny parcels of energy vibrating at different frequencies. The more solid a

---

1. "Greek philosophers, as well as some modern physicists such as Werner Heisenberg, drew their inspiration from ancient Indian philosophies. In *The Positive Sciences of the Ancient Hindus*, Brajendranath Seal explains that the Sankya-Patanjali system of cosmology expresses the fundamental idea of conservation, transformation, and dissipation of energy. Every phenomena in the universe is based on the interaction of intelligence, energy and mass. This is modern physics in a nutshell." Blavatsky, H. (April 1995). 'Ancient and Modern Science'. *Theosophy*, Vol. 83 (issue 6), pp. 169–174. Number 2 of a 7-part series.

thing appears to be, the slower its vibration; the less solid it appears, the faster or finer the vibration. Things exist either as particles, which means that they appear to be solid (like the chair you are sitting on), or as waves, which means that they don't appear to be solid (like light, sound or water). In fact, things can be said to exist – or, more correctly, 'to behave' – as both a wave and a particle at the same time. I will talk more about the particle/wave aspect in Chapter Two.

So, the particles that make up a solid, wooden table have a fairly slow frequency compared to, say, your body, which, being a little less solid than the table, has a finer vibration. And absolutely everything that exists is made up of energy vibrating like this. We already know, for example, that sound is a vibration; we have much technology that works on this basis and is able to measure this vibration. Colour is also a vibration – the difference between colours is simply a difference in frequency[2] – and crystals have a unique kind of frequency.

The space between objects is also energy vibrating very rapidly. In fact, there really is no space and there really are no objects. The whole universe is a kind of 'energy soup' with bits floating around in it all resonating at different frequencies. Those bits look like separate objects to us but they are really just the place where the soup is a bit thicker. This is a very simplistic description of what Lynne McTaggart, author of the fascinating book *The Field*, calls the 'quantum field'. She describes this interconnectivity beautifully, and with another metaphor, when she says "We swim in a sea of light."

If you know anything about quantum theory, you will want to add that the little bits of energy are constantly popping in and

---

2. Colour is simply light of different wavelengths and frequencies and light is just one form of energy made up from photons. We are all surrounded by electromagnetic waves of energy, of which colour is just a small part. See www.colourtherapyhealing.com/colour/

out of existence. I did say that I would not be offering a comprehensive explanation of quantum theory but just those aspects that I have found relevant to coaching. This is one such aspect that is not directly linked to coaching – as yet!

The energy of thoughts

We have established that everything that exists is energy vibrating at different frequencies: solid matter, light, sound, colour, crystals and even our thoughts are a form of vibration. They are a very, very fine vibration of these little bits of energy (another way of describing this is to call it a fine 'energetic vibration') but being fine doesn't mean that they are flimsy. Quite the opposite, in fact: they are extremely powerful.

As coaches, of course, we are keenly aware of the impact of our thoughts and beliefs on our lives and this is a key area for our work with our clients. The quantum skills explain why this is so and I believe that it is extremely helpful for the client to understand this also. When the client has an understanding of the science behind the coaching concepts, and therefore has a grasp of what drives his behaviour and emotional responses, he is far more likely to commit to the actions that he agrees to at the end of his coaching session. I suggest that you tell your clients as much about the tools and techniques of those quantum skills as you can – there is no virtue in making it overly mysterious. Though it is a wonderful mystery indeed.

As we have seen, thoughts are a fine and yet powerful form of energetic vibration. People often tend to think of thoughts as being insubstantial. We say "It's only a thought" as if it's less significant than something more tangible, like an event. This is not the case: a thought can have as much impact on our life as an event and, in fact, may be a critical factor in creating that event. Most quantum physicists agree that, when we think a thought, some key things happen. The first is that the thought, which has properties similar to a magnet (because we are essentially electromagnetic beings), shimmers out into the energy soup and connects with other things in the soup that resonate with it. In other words it attracts things, such as events, that are similar to it. This, very simply put, is how we create the events in our lives. I will cover this in far more detail in Chapter Four, where I will show you how to present this (universal law) to your clients and help them to really grasp it and use it to change the things in their lives that they thought they were stuck with forever.

Another key thing that happens when we think a thought, according to the quantum physicists, is that, as well as shimmering out into, and becoming a part of the energy soup, the thought swims into the energy that is our own body. In the same way that plugging an electrical appliance into a wall socket connects it to the electricity supply allowing the current to flow, our thought connects with every part of our body. It actually flows into the molecules of our body, into the cells, and eventually, if we think a particular kind of thought often enough, into our DNA (Chopra, 1989). In essence, we become what we think. When Descartes said "I think therefore I am", he was describing a very constricted view of our true selves. We often behave as if the truth were "I am what I think." This identification of ourselves with our thoughts is central to the human condition and, although not true either, is the essence of how we limit ourselves. And actually, if we were to explore this fully, it would take us down the spiritual path and show us that our true essence transcends our thoughts (Tolle, 2005). However, the spiritual journey is not the present purpose of this book so, for the moment, we will consider how our thoughts do affect the being that we call 'myself'.

All this is incredibly exciting news for the coach and it begins to be obvious that our physical and mental health and happiness are largely determined by the way we think.

Again, in a later chapter, I describe specific techniques for demonstrating physically to clients that this is how their thoughts affect their body and for helping them to really take responsibility for how they allow themselves to think. The theories are endlessly fascinating, but it is only when clients actually feel the physical sensation of these concepts materialising and happening in their own body that they will believe it sufficiently to build it into their daily life. We all know how we can become enthralled with a new idea but somehow lose touch with it within a very short time. I will describe a series of exercises and challenges that will help you to help your clients embed these ideas into their belief systems so that they will quickly become habits. As well as being for the benefit of clients, of course, it is vital that we, as coaches, also implement these tools and techniques in our own lives. We cannot hope to convince clients that this is life-changing stuff unless it is our own daily experience.

So, these are just a couple of the threads of quantum theory that are woven into the quantum skills for coaches process. There are others, which I will describe as we go along.

CHAPTER TWO

Where do the quantum skills for coaches come from?

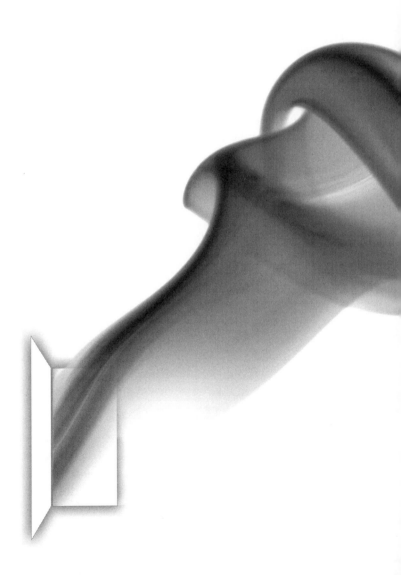

The concept that I am calling quantum skills for coaches has emerged for me over the past fifteen years from a variety of component concepts, theories and processes. Some of these are drawn from books that I have studied over the years and some from my own personal experiences or my experiences in working with others. However, they all have a common thread in that, in some way, they relate to energy as I defined it in the first chapter.

The quantum skills have been emerging so gradually that, for a long while, I didn't recognise them as being an identifiable form of coaching. I used to describe the way I work as a coach as being 'a bit weird' and, if pushed, I would call it 'process coaching'. Nevertheless, I found the process that I used astonishing in its simplicity and potency. I have been continually amazed by the way in which I keep discovering that the concepts and processes with which other people are working give me new insights into what I am doing and confirm the validity of approaching human issues in this way. It is like a cloth being created – continually growing as each new facet of the same truth is woven into the fabric.

Co-Active Coaching by Laura Whitworth, Henry Kimsey-House and Phil Sandahl describes a form of 'process coaching' that influenced and encouraged me to experiment with this approach. Several other influences are books that teach specific techniques, such as *Focusing*, by Eugene Gendlin, *The Journey*, by Brandon Bays, and *Self-Powerment*, by Faye Mandell, which were thrilling to read and in many ways similar to each other and similar to what I was doing. When I read them, I recognised the essence of what the authors were saying and extracted that essence to enrich my own coaching practice.

I found, however, that working with the specific step-by-step set of techniques that these marvellous books outline did not correspond to the way I work, which is to remain totally open and fluid to the path that the session takes and to be led by the client at all times. If during 'step two' of a particular technique, for example, the client does not answer in the way that is needed to take us smoothly to 'step three', it could produce an interruption in the process.

Even though I do not follow their processes to the letter, all of these books were immensely influential in shaping the quantum skills tool kit. I feel it will be helpful to include a description of these different influences here so that, if you want to really gain a full picture of the roots of these quantum skills for coaches, you can read the books or explore the sources for yourself.

The central origins of the quantum skills for coaches, in approximately the chronological order in which I met them, are:

- My 'well of pain' experience
- Being 'in the present moment'
- Focusing
- Quantum physics
- Reiki
- Creative visualisation
- Psychodrama
- Cognitive behaviour therapy.

My 'well of pain' experience

As I trace the journey back to my first awareness of applying a process akin to those that eventually became the quantum skill set, I am in my mid-thirties and the mother of three children, the youngest of whom is two years old. As she reached this age, no longer a baby but now a little girl, this triggered in me one morning a cataclysmic unleashing of an inner knowing: now was the time that I had to deal with the fact that, as a child and an adolescent, I had been sexually abused by my stepfather. I had always known it and hadn't buried it exactly, but I had never really looked at it full in the face and worked through it. Although I had felt angry with him and with my mother, I had accommodated it into my life reasonably easily and with no drama. Now it all changed. One morning I woke up to see a huge metaphorical fist clenched in my face and there was no escape. 'Deal with it – now!' was the challenge.

I collapsed into tears and wept as if I would never stop. Fortunately, a wise friend was at hand and she helped me through this crisis by teaching me a process for handling this kind of emotional pain. Although at the time I did not know it, this process was very much a foundation for the use of quantum skills in coaching, and one that I would later pass on to others in a variety of personal development training courses.

My friend told me to feel the pain until I became used to how it felt and then go deeper into it and feel the new level. This is how I did it.

Each day when the house was empty, my then husband was at work, my two sons were at school and my infant daughter was having a nap, I would choose to go into the pain and feel it for what it was, rather like going down into a deep, deep well where the pain lived. It was intense and I would sob, punch pillows and do whatever came naturally but I didn't consciously think about what had happened with my brain or process it in any way. This was the critical element in the process. I just sat in the experience – in this 'well of emotional pain' – and felt the physical sensation of the pain in my body.

It was astonishing to discover, or at least be consciously aware of the fact, that an emotion can be experienced in a tangible, physical way. When visual images of particular episodes of the abuse came creeping into my mind, I didn't focus in on the detail of what had happened but neither did I resist the memory. I let the visual picture play itself out and produce whatever spontaneous emotion it chose, and I put my attention on this emotion rather than allow my mind to produce any internal commentary on it. This may sound a little strange described in words but, once you realise that it is possible to focus on the physical sensation of an emotion, you will understand how it feels to do so. (We will look at how to do this in Chapter Eight.)

After around thirty minutes to an hour of being in this painful place, when I felt that I had done enough work on it for the time being, I would choose to end the session, 'climb out of the well' into the real world and get on with the rest of the day. The following day, I would go down into the well again and, because the pain level that I had experienced the day before was now familiar and slightly less intense, I could choose to descend a little deeper this time and experience the new level. Still feeling it in my body and not allowing myself to think thoughts about it or engage my brain in any way, I would sob my way through this level of pain and then emerge from the well once more, go shopping, make the supper, take my daughter for a walk or do whatever was needed for the family.

Once I had re-emerged into the world, did I suddenly click back into cheerful normality as if nothing was going on inside me? No, I knew that I was experiencing an ongoing process that would take me however long was necessary to work through it. Outside of the well, I was peaceful, sad, trusting, open and from time to time a little tearful. However, the tears, if they came, never overtook me or dragged me back into the well against my will and I had no fear that they would. It felt empowering and important that it was always I who chose the moments for my descent into the well – they never chose me.

I told my husband what I was working through but didn't discuss it with him. And I would go and see my friend from time to time to tell her how I was getting on but not to talk about the abuse. It was almost as if she was there for me, waiting at the top of the well with a virtual cup of tea when I came out of the pain, but the work itself was solo. I couldn't take her down into the well with me to help me through this. I had to simply feel the pain and let my body deal with it in its own time and in its own miraculous way. If I had started analysing it with my head, commenting on what I thought about it or working out what to do about it, I believe I may still be doing it today.

The powerful thing about working with the agony in this way was that *I felt totally safe*. I was in control of my own process and at no time did I feel that it might be stronger than me or take me anywhere where I would be unable to cope. There was no danger of spiralling out of control. This immense trust in the process is a highly significant feature of what we now call quantum skills for coaches.

After about six months of diligently doing this work and going deeper and deeper into my own pain, I eventually reached a place where it didn't hurt any longer. It was not that it was numbed but rather that it was neutralised. It was like a serpent that had been defanged and had no further power over me to make me suffer. We might call it healing. Whenever I remembered the abuse, it didn't produce the slightest shiver of revulsion or anger within me – and it has been that way ever since.

This was my first experience of consciously dealing with pain in this way, although I think that I, and probably most of us, may have unconsciously done this many times and been unaware of it.

Being 'in the present moment'

It wasn't until years later when I came across Deepak Chopra's description of managing emotional pain in his book, *Ageless Body, Timeless Mind*, that I realised that the reason why my 'well of pain' experience had been so successful was that when I was down in the 'well' I was totally immersed in the present moment. Although the issue I had been dealing with took place in the past, I wasn't reliving those past experiences when I was in the well: I was feeling the sensations that the experiences caused me to feel *and these sensations were in the present moment*. Chopra said "Our feelings are the most present-centred thing we have."

I was in a healing process and all healing takes place in the present moment. It is our thoughts that take us out of the present – either into the past where we dredge up stuff and get angry or guilty about it, or into the future where we feel anxious or fearful about what might happen. When we simply feel the feelings and choose not to engage our brain in thoughts about the issue, our bodies can work powerfully, simply and with a clarity that leaves our brains wide-eyed with amazement.

This aspect of the quantum skills for coaches – being in the moment – is a key feature of the process and over the years I have learned more and more about the importance of being in this sacred and magical place. One of the most significant proponents of being in the moment is Eckhart Tolle, whose wonderful book *The Power of Now* continues to have a major impact on my life and work and is a text that I frequently recommend to coaching clients.

Confirmation from Chopra and Tolle that the 'well of pain' process was valid motivated me to pass this technique onto others when running personal development workshops. I would often receive letters from workshop participants, months after a course, saying they'd "been doing the well of pain thing and had finally emerged smiling". With each such letter, I received an exciting reconfirmation that this technique somehow transcends levels of human suffering and pain and connects with our innate ability to heal ourselves.

Focusing

Focusing is the name of a technique that Eugene Gendlin describes in his book of the same name. The technique involves experiencing the physicality of an emotional event while disengaging the mind and thus allowing the wisdom within the body itself to deal with the underlying issue. It is essentially the process I discovered while in my 'well of pain' and which appears in the work of Deepak Chopra, Eckhart Tolle, Tara Bennett-Goleman and many others. It is really another aspect of 'being in the present moment', which means that these first three elements (being in the well of pain, being in the present moment and focusing) are really just different features of the same thing. Focusing is a core element of quantum skills, although the way I will teach you to use it is less structured than in Eugene Gendlin's book. I describe it in full detail in Chapter Eight.

Quantum physics

I have already introduced some of the theories uncovered by quantum physics, which was clearly a key element in developing, describing and finally naming these quantum skills for coaches. Among the significant books that I read as I first discovered quantum physics were Dana Zohar's *The Quantum Self*, Deepak Chopra's *Quantum Healing* and *Ageless Body, Timeless Mind*, Amit Goswami's *Self Aware Universe* and *The Quantum Doctor*, Robert Gilmore's *Alice in Quantumland* and Lynne McTaggart's *The Field*, as well as a host of papers and articles on the subject. More recently, the book and film *What the Bleep Do We Know* and *Down the Rabbit Hole* have articulated the beliefs of many scientists and doctors, including Amit Goswami, John Hagelin, Candace Pert, Fred Alan Wolf, Joe Dispenza, Masaru Emoto, Stuart Hameroff, Daniel Monti, Andrew Newberg, William Tiller and Ervin Laszlo, about the significance of quantum physics to the way we live our lives.

What I loved about quantum physics was that it explained in scientific terms so many things that seemed to be 'wacky' and 'out there', and offered rigorous scientific evidence and research to substantiate concepts that might be considered unbelievable. As I continued to explore the implications of working with energy in a business context as a management consultant, coach and trainer, I was able to show my clients the 'wacky and weird' but describe it as 'what modern science is now saying', which meant that more people would pay attention to it and use the tools and techniques I designed. Those who did use the tools saw amazing results from their coaching programmes and this continued to encourage me to explore it even further.

There are many fascinating experiments in quantum physics that make people sit up and pay attention, and which demonstrate simply and elegantly how this aspect of science can be applied to our day-to-day-lives. The following experiment is one that I always find particularly compelling. If you find any form of science a turn-off, then you can skip the next five paragraphs (and doing so won't affect your ability to learn quantum coaching skills).

Quantum theory shows that matter (i.e. objects that we can see) can exist in two possible states. It may either take the form of particles and appear as a solid object, or take the form of waves, as we saw earlier in this chapter, and appear in a non-solid form (such as light, sound, magnetism or heat). Taken a little further, the theory also says that matter actually exists in *both of these states* simultaneously until the act of observing it holds it in a single state. Wow!

The experiment simply described (remember, I am not a physicist) is to take a kind of screen with two slits in it. If you send a photon (a tiny quantity) of light in the form of a particle through the screen, it will pass through one slit only. If it exists in the form of a wave, it will flow through both slits. Of course the photon is too small to actually be seen so the only way to tell whether it has passed through the screen as a particle is to have a particle detector on the other side of the screen. And likewise, you need a wave detector in place on the other side to tell if it has passed through as a wave.

You would set up the experiment as follows. (This is a much-simplified version of an experiment that has more layers than this but, for the purposes of understanding its essence, this description is sufficient.) You have a photon generator on one side of the screen and a particle detector on the other side and you generate and send a photon through the screen. What happens? The detector shows that it has passed through one slit in the form of a particle. Ok so far? So then you exchange the particle detector for the wave detector and repeat the exercise. What happens this time? Hmmm . . . The photon is detected by the wave detector – so it passed through the screen as a wave. We could also say that it has 'behaved like a wave'.

What does this mean? It means that the photon *seems to know what is on the other side of the screen*. It obviously cannot see the detector but it seems to know it is there and it complies with the intent of the experiment. It does what is expected of it. The very presence of the wave detector means that the experimenter expects the photon to behave like a wave and so it does.

Heavens above! What does this mean? It means, according to the scientists, that *the photon appears to read the intent of the experimenter*. It means that the intent, or perhaps we should call it 'the consciousness', of the person conducting the experiment is a part of the variables of it and affects the outcome. Fritjof Capra, author of *The Tao of Physics*, wrote:

> "My conscious decision about how to observe an electron will determine the electron's properties to some extent. If I ask it a particle question, it will give me a particle answer. If I ask it a wave question, it will give me a wave answer."

This is exciting news indeed, with implications that reach into every part of our lives. So, when quantum physics states that everything is energy (and I once heard Deepak Chopra say "everything is spirit", which is a non-scientific way of saying the same thing), it means *everything*. Every 'thing' that can be preceded by the word 'the' is energy. Therefore '*the* intent' of the experimenter is a form of energy. Every single thing that goes into the 'energy soup' that we talked about in the last chapter is connected to everything else in the soup. Deepak Chopra calls the energy soup the "field of potentiality", which gives an additional slant on its capability.

An implication of this experiment with the photon (and one that is not connected to coaching but is interesting all the same) is that no experiment, however rigorously scientific can be detached from the intent of the experimenter. In some way the elements of the experiment will collude to give the expected result, so this has to be factored into the design of the experiment by, for example, using a 'control group'. So, the standard scientific methodology, where a scientist develops a hypothesis about something and then designs an experiment to prove it, has already influenced the outcome in his favour.[3]

If we continue this discussion further we will find ourselves embarking upon an exploration of the nature of consciousness and spirituality. While this would be fascinating and

---

3. "Heisenberg's great contribution to modern quantum theory was the "uncertainty principle." Simply stated, the observer alters the observed by the mere act of observation. The "uncertainty principle" mathematically measures that degree to which he influences the outcome of an experiment. The outcome is affected because the observer is a participant in the event. Researchers affect observations and outcomes through the measurement devices they choose and how they use those devices. Quantum theory reveals the interdependence and relationship between the various parts and the whole of nature, between the observer and the observed, between the individual and the universe." Blavatsky, H. (April 1995). 'Ancient and Modern Science'. *Theosophy*, Vol. 83 (issue 6), pp. 169–174. Number 2 of a 7-part series.

worthwhile it would take us rather off course at this point, as I am simply trying to show the connection between quantum physics and the coaching techniques I have developed.

Let us consider further this field of potentiality into which we drop our intent – not just in scientific experiments but also in any other situation in our lives. Say, for example, you want to give a colleague some feedback on his recent presentation to a new client, and you have found the words that convey this in positive terms – at least you think you have.

If, in reality, you have an unconscious desire to put him down because, in the secret recesses of your heart you feel that he is competing with you, then this is your actual intent. It is the covert intent *behind* your intent. And it is through the filter of this covert intent that your words will be uttered. Even if you select just the right words to give supportive feedback something will happen in the uttering, that will convey your real intent and the person will feel diminished. It may be a nuance of the tone of your voice or the little muscles around your eyes that give you away. He may not be able to put his finger on exactly why he feels diminished but he will sense it and will feel untrusting towards you, thus helping to create the very friction with him that you fear. This is why it is vital for you in your role as a coach to identify your true intent and for you to help your clients to identify theirs in situations that prove challenging.

We drop our intent into the field of potentiality like a stone into a pond. The ripples flow outward connecting with, and affecting, everything around it. The power of our intent in any given situation is a force to be recognised and scrutinised with pure honesty if we are to achieve what we hope to achieve in our lives. The way the power of intent operates is a natural law – it is one of the implications of quantum physics and will always function like this in any situation. It is how the world works. Another way of describing this is to call it a 'natural law of the universe'. There are several such natural laws of the universe that I will cover throughout this book and then summarise in Chapter Twenty. The world will always operate according to these laws, whether we recognise them as being valid or not.

One could define wisdom as understanding how the world works and working with it to get the results that you want. The power of intent is like this. If you understand how it works and scrutinise your intent before acting, you are more likely to achieve the outcome you desire than if you kid yourself about your true intent. As we can see from the example of giving someone feedback on their presentation, kidding yourself about your intent will lead to your helping to create a flawed relationship with the other person, which will continue to create problems for both of you in the future.

As human beings, our intent is one of the most powerful factors in any situation (not to mention one of the most powerful forces in the universe) and when we truly understand how to work with it, it becomes one of the most powerful tools available to us. And, of course, as a coach, it is one of the most powerful tools that you can offer your clients.

Reiki

The fourth source from which the quantum skills for coaches has emerged was from my awareness of the energetic nature of all things as I practised the hands-on healing technique called 'reiki'. I am sure that most of you have heard of reiki, and many probably practise it, so I won't give a detailed explanation of it here. Briefly, though, it is a powerful technique for healing, relaxation and stress reduction, which works through channelling the 'universal life force' (which is what the word 'reiki' means) and can be practised by anyone. It is not learned in the usual sense but is passed from a master to a student in an 'attunement ritual'. If you haven't heard of it, there is a wealth of information about it in books and on the internet. (See, for example, www.reiki.org)

When I first encountered reiki, it added another layer of interest to my understanding of quantum physics and confirmed the notion that energy flows through all living things and that we are all connected to each other through the 'energy soup' or energy flow. I have been a reiki master for about twelve years, which means that I am able to 'attune' another person to reiki enabling them to practise it too.

Reiki is becoming increasingly accepted by, and used in, mainstream medicine. Used in conjunction with conventional cancer treatments, it is reported to ease the side effects of chemotherapy and radiation, improve immune function, ease anxiety and enhance positive emotional attitude, decrease pain and promote relaxation. There are ongoing clinical trials of reiki healing techniques for diabetic peripheral vascular disease and autonomic neuropathy, carried out at the University of Michigan Taubman Health Care Center. The Center for Research in Complementary and Alternative Medicine for Stroke and Neurological Disorders at the Kessler Institute for Rehabilitation in West Orange, New Jersey, has a research programme into rehabilitation from a stroke, spinal cord injury and traumatic brain injury, using reiki. In the USA there are over a hundred hospitals that now use reiki, of which the following are just a few:

Bayonne Hospital, New Jersey

California Pacific Medical Center — one of the largest hospitals in northern California

Columbia Medical Center, New York

Complementary Medical Center, Windsor Hospital, Vermont

Foote Hospital in Jackson, Mississippi

Marin General Hospital in Marin County, California

Memorial Sloan-Kettering Hospital, New York

Mercy Hospital in Cincinnati, Ohio

Portsmouth Regional Hospital, Portsmouth, New Hampshire

St. Luke's Women's Care, Cedar Rapids, Iowa

University of Pennsylvania Medical School.

The fact that reiki is being practised in so many significant medical establishments further substantiates the notion that it is possible to work with energy in a practical way to produce tangible and measurable results.

Creative visualisation

I described earlier how the quantum soup or field of potentiality connects all things and how this makes the power of our intent so potent. Visualisation connects principally with the 'Law of Attraction' and is a wonderfully practical way of working with this natural law to get the results in your life that you desire. This also restates our earlier definition of wisdom – understanding how the world works and working with it to get the results that you want. One of the best books I have read on this subject is Shakti Gawain's *Creative Visualisation*, and I would warmly recommend it to you as I do to any clients to whom I introduce visualisation and who want to learn more about it.

Creative visualisation works on the principle that the universe is like a vast copying machine. When we send a thought (or an intent) out into the field of potentiality, it connects with the field and, having qualities rather like a magnet, attracts towards it things that are similar to it. So, when we say to ourselves "I don't think I want to work with this company any more", the universe will produce the circumstances that will eventually produce this situation – maybe we get freed by getting fired!

In Chapter Four I will give you a detailed process for introducing a visualisation technique to your client, and in Chapter Twenty I talk a little more about how this and other universal laws link to the coaching process.

Psychodrama

This is a type of drama therapy conceived and developed by Jacob L. Moreno in which the therapist helps the client to explore their issues using guided dramatic action. It can be used with groups, such as families, as well as with individuals. A number of years ago I took a foundation course in psychodrama and was amazed at the power of the role-play techniques and group dynamic processes I learned, which enable the client to gain insights into deeply embedded issues and understand them on both a cognitive and emotional level. The techniques help the client to gently integrate aspects of themselves that have been damaged in the past, leading to effective behaviour change.

From this basic training I learned much about how to access understanding of our problems and traumas by stepping outside our own perception of the issue. We can do this either by working within our body and allowing the wisdom of our body to speak to us, or working with the perceptions of other people or even inanimate objects in the situation.

I frequently use psychodrama-based techniques in coaching sessions and see it as a wonderful tool for helping the client to explore an issue by leaving their usual mindset and, sometimes even playfully, looking at it from a different angle. The way I typically use this approach is to ask the client to put himself in the shoes of one of the aspects of the issue and get a sense of how the issue looks from this new viewpoint. However, in the same way that I extract the essence from other techniques, such as focusing and 'the journey', as I mentioned earlier, I do not necessarily follow the psychodrama process to the letter but allow it to go where it will – often combining it with techniques similar to focusing and 'the journey'. Sometimes this leads to the client engaging in a conversation with this aspect or perhaps even allowing two aspects to have a conversation with each other about the issue. You will find a case study illustrating the use of this tool in Chapter Nineteen.

Cognitive behaviour therapy

Although cognitive behaviour therapy (CBT) is not really an aspect of quantum skills for coaches, I am including it here because it uses very similar concepts. When I came across CBT, I immediately realised that this form of psychotherapy had much in common with the ideas I was working with and developing. Since coaching is not therapy, I am not going to suggest that you should learn cognitive behavior therapy, but it is useful to understand a little about it. However, it is also true to say that there are some CBT training bodies that actually do teach CBT alongside coaching.

This breakthrough in mental health care, which we now call cognitive behaviour therapy, dates back to the sixties and stems from the work of Aaron T. Beck, an American psychiatrist and psychotherapist. The volumes of research studies undertaken since then show why CBT is increasingly becoming the preferred treatment of many psychologists and psychiatrists for a variety of conditions such as depression and mood swings, shyness and social anxiety, panic attacks and phobias, obsessions and compulsions, chronic anxiety or worry, post-traumatic stress symptoms, eating disorders, insomnia, difficulty in maintaining relationships, etc.

The central idea in cognitive therapy is that our thoughts arise from stimuli such as external events and these create our emotions. So it is not the event itself that directly creates an emotional response, but our interpretation of that event or our thoughts about it.

There are two main assumptions in the practice of the therapy. Firstly, clients are capable of becoming aware of their own thoughts and of changing them. And secondly, sometimes the thoughts created by the event or stimulus either distort reality or fail to reflect it accurately.

The emotions created in this way drive our behaviour and the behavioural patterns thus formed create situations in our lives. When the cycle – stimulus → thought → emotion → behaviour – is negative in its nature, then the events created by the behaviours tend to be negative and reinforce the negative thoughts that create the emotions.

Cognitive therapy helps the client initially to become aware of the thought distortions that cause psychological distress, as well as the behavioural patterns reinforcing it. The therapist then helps to correct both of these by teaching the client to practise mindfulness, which facilitates a change in the unhelpful behaviour patterns, and works extensively with the client's personal values in much the same way as a coach does.

This chapter has given an overview of the various elements that have shaped quantum skills for coaches and which we will explore more fully in subsequent chapters. Quantum skills have emerged from the following influences, which, although quite different, are all interconnected in that they relate to energy.

- In my 'well of pain' experience I was able to move through intense emotional pain by choosing to 'be in the pain' and feeling the sensation until it was neutralised and ultimately healed.

- 'Being in the moment' reinforces this well of pain process since, when we feel the sensation of an emotion, we are always in the present moment. When we go 'into our head' and think about the emotion, it takes us out of the moment and into the past or the future, thus preventing us from working through the emotion.

- The focusing process engages the wisdom inherent in the physical body to explore an issue by working with the feeling generated by our emotional response to the issue.

- Research in the field of quantum physics tells us that everything is energy and reveals a great deal about the natural laws that govern the world we live in. One of these is the 'Law of Intent', which shows that our true intent in a situation will strongly affect the outcome of our actions.

- Reiki is a hands-on healing, relaxation and stress reduction technique, which works by channelling the universal life force – the energy of which everything is made – into the person being treated.

- Creative visualisation techniques are a powerful method for creating the events we desire in our lives using the natural 'Law of Attraction'.

- Psychodrama is a tool for exploring an issue by stepping out from behind your own viewpoint and looking at it from other angles.

- Cognitive behaviour therapy helps us to be more in control of the stimulus→thought→emotion→behaviour cycle in the treatment of psychological problems.

CHAPTER THREE

Aren't you breaking the 'rules of coaching'?

You may be thinking that all this does sound a little as if it takes coaching into the arena of therapy and, indeed, this is a question I have asked myself extensively and struggled with over the years. The argument below is one that I finally accepted, with the help of several past clients, when I shared these concerns with them.

A second question that I have asked myself about the coaching techniques I use is about the role of the coach as an advisor. As we know from our training as coaches and from the literature we have studied about coaching, the coach is not supposed to offer advice to the client. However, a major aspect of the quantum skills is the 'tool kit' of techniques, concepts and ways of looking at the world that I offer my clients. When I first started coaching I was reluctant to do this lest it seem like advice. But because clients continually confirmed, verbally and in writing, that these tools were invaluable to them I continued to offer this tool kit and have allowed it to develop.

So, now, before I share the tool kit with you, I would just like to address these two questions about the validity of breaking these rules of coaching: are we stepping over the boundary and should coaches give advice?

Are we stepping over the coaching boundary and into therapy?

To explore the implications of this, we will ask the questions: 'What is therapy?' and "Can something be therapeutic without being 'therapy'?" First, though, we will clarify what we understand coaching to be and what it is not.

Coaching, as we know, is about helping clients to find their own solutions. This is done firstly through deep-veined listening where the coach is able to listen, not only to the words the client utters but also to the way they are uttered. This enables the coach to pick up on 'the music behind the words' and tune into realities that the client may be describing but is perhaps not consciously aware of, and which may provide clues with which the coach can work. The other key skill in coaching is the use of powerful and incisive questions, which help clients to see situations in new ways and cut through their limiting assumptions about 'the way things are.'

An essential component of successful coaching is that coaches adopt a 'coaching mindset', which means firstly that they have no attachment to their own agenda and secondly that they see everything that clients say merely as information with which to work, with no judgement as to whether it is good or bad, desirable or not.

This, I think you will agree, is a fairly simple overview of the essence of coaching. As coaches, we have also been well-drilled in an understanding of what coaching is not through our training programmes and the books we have studied: it is not advising, counselling or therapy. All the input comes from the client and not from us. We might offer feedback as to what we observe in the client's behaviour, body language or responses but this really is the limit of our input.

I believe that most coaches, at some time or another, disregard this when we feel it to be appropriate. For instance, if the client is totally disorganised it would be a bit of a struggle to coach them into designing an effective time-management tool from scratch. We clearly want to hear their thoughts about the way they manage their time and what being organised might look like to them but, with scores of books on time management to draw from, it generally feels acceptable to give them a heads-up on one of the many effective and proven techniques available, or at least some 'hot hints and tips' on being more organised. Similarly, when coaching a client through managing stress, how many coaches would think twice about teaching a deep breathing exercise?

And then, as we explore the issues that are causing the stress, what happens if we discover that the client is experiencing some deep emotional pain? Do we back off at that point and refer the client to a therapist or do we explore further with the client? What if our further explorations reveal that the client is terrified of creating authentic relationships with others? Do we then cease the coaching programme? If we continue and find that this fear is rooted in a dysfunctional childhood, does that ring the warning bells for us?

You may have found yourself trying to answer any of these questions at some point in your coaching experiences and come up with different answers at different times, depending on the client and your feeling of confidence at that moment. The truth is that we're making judgements about these things all the time and using our intuition to decide what to do. People are holistic beings and every part of their life is connected to every other part.

You may be coaching a senior executive to develop leadership skills to improve team performance and, in the process, uncover feelings of inferiority around others caused by a dominant father. The executive's workplace issues are securely linked to this and to try to deal with the leadership skills without addressing the impact of the parent's behaviour is to apply a sticking plaster to an infected wound without first cleansing it. You may ask yourself "What if I open a Pandora's box?" What if you do not? The client will always be at risk from the lid popping open at some other time and releasing the emotions that have been suppressed for so long. An advertisement on a passing bus, a film or television programme or a throwaway comment overheard in the company cafeteria can release the fragile catch on the box. The question is how to do it in a way that is safe and leads to permanent change?

Therapy or not?

The key word is 'therapy' – we know that we are not supposed to cross the line between coaching and therapy. What is therapy, then? Back to dictionary-type definitions!

1. *A treatment of physical, mental, or behavioural problems that is meant to cure or rehabilitate somebody*
2. *Psychoanalysis or techniques from another school of psychotherapy, intended to treat mental and emotional problems with psychological methods.*

The second definition points towards the work of a professionally qualified psychotherapist. In the first definition, the words 'treatment' and 'cure' might be significant here so let's look those up too.

Treatment:

1. *The application of medical care to cure disease, heal injuries, or ease symptoms*
2. *A particular remedy, procedure, or technique for curing or alleviating a disease, injury, or condition.*

Cure:

1. *To restore a sick person or animal to health*
2. *To bring about recovery from an illness, disorder, or injury.*

And, while we've got the dictionary out, 'to recover' is:

1. *To return to a previous state of health, prosperity, or equanimity*
2. *To bring the self back to a normal condition.*

While all of these definitions refer primarily to professional medical intervention, they all also point to a more general restoration of normal functioning. Therapy could be described as 'applying a technique or set of tools' as, indeed, is CBT. At the beginning of this chapter, I proffered the question "Can something be therapeutic without being 'therapy'?" An overview of the above definitions shows that therapy can be seen as *applying a technique to alleviate a condition and bring the self back to a normal condition or to return someone to a previous state of health or equanimity*. Therefore, an activity that achieves this outcome could be seen to be therapeutic.

We all know that when we're feeling negative, stressed or even depressed a walk in the woods, a swim in the sea, cleaning the house, baking a loaf of bread or planning a new project such as moving house all help to move us to a more positive place of equanimity. These activities can be described as therapeutic. And, of course, we all know that retail therapy is aptly named! When we are troubled, just talking to someone about the problem can feel like therapy. If I ask a room of coaches "Do your clients ever give you the feedback that they have found a coaching session to be therapeutic?", almost all raise their hands.

Yes, but is it safe?

So, it is not totally outrageous to consider that coaching can be a therapeutic experience for our client. The question, then, is how appropriate and safe is it to venture into areas that we have been taught are off-limits for the coach – mood swings, depression, shyness, social anxiety, feeling stressed out, panic attacks, phobias, obsessions and compulsions, chronic anxiety, eating disorders, difficulty in maintaining relationships, inadequate coping skills, over-inhibition of feelings or expression, etc. This list is very similar to the list of conditions, which I showed in the previous chapter, that cognitive behaviour therapy is typically used to treat.

My experience, and that of colleagues who work with the quantum skills for coaches, is that, while we would not advertise ourselves as coaches who work with clients in these areas, if such issues do emerge during a coaching programme, then the coach will carefully consider whether to continue. I tend to tell the client that "Coaching does not usually cover this area but, that having said that, I work with a process that uses the wisdom of the body to surface the 'inner knowing' housed in the body." I share with the client further details about the quantum skills and the body-mind, (a concept described in Chapter Nine) and a little about the specific techniques for focusing on our personal issues within our body.

I believe that, when we deal with such problems in this way, we are far safer than if we attempt to work them out using our brain with its reasoning and logic. My own experience sixteen years ago in the 'well of pain' was my first inkling of this, and the many experiences I have since witnessed as I have shared this method with others has continued to confirm that this is the case. I will continue to give examples of why I believe this to be true throughout this book.

Once I have had this conversation, I leave it with the client to decide whether to consult a therapist specialising in the issue or continue to work with the quantum skills process. By this time, the client and I have a solid coaching relationship and the client trusts the way I work. Because of this, all such clients have so far chosen to explore their issue in our sessions. However, I would be genuinely happy if they opted to talk to a therapist instead.

Many clients have also told me that the reason they feel so comfortable to examine their 'hot buttons' with me is that my utter confidence and conviction in the safety and naturalness of the process makes them feel safe with it – and if I were less certain, this would affect their decision to do so. I never guarantee results, of course, but I do firmly believe that whatever comes out of the exploration will be helpful. In Chapter Eight in particular, and in many other sections of this book, I explain in greater detail why I have such confidence in this process and why I believe that, when you go within and allow your body to 'look at' an issue, you are safer than when you examine it with reason, logic and the need to understand by thinking with your mind.

Are coaches supposed to give advice?

This is the second question that challenged me as I developed the quantum skills for coaches process and found myself offering my clients a growing tool kit of techniques, ideas and concepts, which I felt were invaluable, about 'the way things work'. However, this is not to say that every time I coach a client I will refer to this tool kit. Sometimes I will stick with the standard coaching methodology of asking powerful questions to explore the way the client sees their issue, challenging their limiting beliefs about it, generating options for moving forward and getting them to commit to make the change in their behaviour or attitude.

This standard methodology is known as the GROW model. Sometimes, within this process, I will dip into my kit and pull out a tool to use and then continue with the session in the standard way. But, since many of the tools in my kit do involve the coach sharing information with the client, I found that my thinking around this question returned to my earlier definition of wisdom as understanding how the world works and working with it to get the results that you want. Not, you understand, that I feel I have pinned wisdom down to a few facile techniques. Far from it! And this is the point actually.

I believe that the main reasons we are here on earth are to be happy and to become the finest version of ourselves that we are able to be. To achieve these goals, we need to learn and grow and there are certain natural laws (which I have already referred to) that provide us with some guidelines for this growth and learning. Most of the tools in our quantum skills tool kit are derived from these natural laws of the universe, which simply tell us how things work. In the same way that gravity and magnetism are laws of physics, these laws describe the way things work from an energy-based and a 'consciousness-aware' point of view. 'Energy-based' because they work with the theory that everything is made of energy and 'consciousness-aware' because they touch on the vast power inherent in 'being'.

As I said earlier, to begin to explore the nature of consciousness would take us into the realms of spirituality and away from the pragmatic objective of this book. Of course, I cannot deny that this is the pathway down which these ideas ultimately lead, but the book is about the link between quantum theory and coaching and not essentially about spiritual coaching. Quantum theory has clear threads connecting it to a study of consciousness and spirituality; if you are interested in exploring this, you will enjoy the film *What the Bleep Do We Know?* and the website www.whatthebleep.com. There are many coaches who specialise in spiritual coaching and sometimes, if this is where a client states that they wish to go in their programme, I am delighted to go with them into this arena. But to teach you to be a spiritual coach is not the aim of this book.

Let's get back to the natural laws and the tool kit. Since the tool kit is formed around the natural laws, I can honestly say that this is not just some stuff I made up and which makes me look clever. If it were, goodness me, I would never have the confidence to base my coaching around it and take others at their most vulnerable into this flimsy construct. No, it is because the tools in the kit are so assuredly founded on powerful, universal and totally mind-blowing truths that I am able to give the client a sense of safety and solidity when I talk about them. In fact, when I first began working with the tools and had little evidence of their effectiveness other than in my own life, I was still able to give the same sense of certainty when I described them to my new clients. It was as if my inner knowing trusted these tools already and I can still remember wondering why it was that I felt so sure that they would be effective. I now believe that, at that time, I was given a special gift to trust in the tools – and I did.

The tool kit, as well as being a practical set of techniques that clients can apply to their lives to support the changes that they wish to make, is also intended as an explanation of how the natural laws work. This is very important because we are not asking the client to blindly carry out certain techniques trusting in the superior understanding of the coach to comprehend their mystery and meaning. As a coach, I want my clients to understand as much as possible about the philosophy and theory of the tools I am using; when they are so thrilled with the results they see that they want to share their understanding with family or friends, then I am delighted. Understanding and applying the tools (I also think of them as toys because they are quite conducive to play) can help us to become the best version of who we really are and thus feel happier. This is our birthright – to step into the castle that we are – and the more people who know how to tap into this source of wellbeing the better for all of us.

I see the 'human condition' as a set of challenges that are fairly generic and which we, as human beings, typically face on our life journey, as I am sure you have found in your coaching practice. Fear of failure or rejection, of looking stupid or incompetent and difficulties in sustaining fulfilling relationships of all kinds are just a few of these challenges. This is not to say that we are simplifying the complexity of humanity into a list of typical problems, but these are the places in our psyches where our challenges tend to appear. From a spiritual perspective, you might use a phrase such as "Where there is fear, there is an absence of love" to describe the human condition. But, whatever the source of these generic challenges, as coaches, we believe that the client has the answer within them but doesn't know it. The natural laws or the spiritual laws of the universe, whatever you prefer to call them, are the articulation of this knowing and this is the reason for adapting these laws into a tool kit. Most of the generic issues will be answered through understanding and applying these laws.

As we have just seen, although at some instinctive level within us we already know these natural laws, most of us do not know that we know them. They have either worked for us or against us (depending upon the actions we have chosen) all our lives but we have never articulated them or applied them consciously. When we hear someone describe them to us in words, it is as if we recognise them from a distant past. Once we hear these things, we can then apply them to our lives intentionally and start to see the results we desire. People often say "I always knew that" when I describe the tools to them – it's a process of remembering.

PART TWO

The Tool Kit

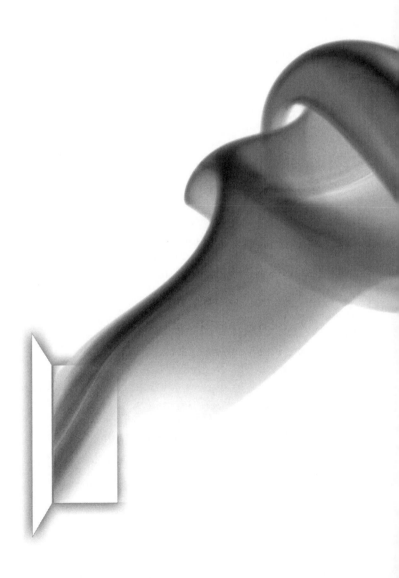

Introduction

The next five chapters describe the tool kit that I have referred to so many times. Now I don't want you to think that once you have worked your way through it you should use it all the time and abandon the great tried and tested coaching methods you have been using successfully for so long. As I said in the last chapter, I will often coach someone using GROW or a similar coaching model and ask a series of simple, powerful questions to explore the client's perceptions, values, feelings and ideas about solutions to the issue that we are dealing with. It is when I intuitively sense that there is something going on with the client and this would benefit from the application of a little quantum 'magic' (I jest of course, but the tools can appear to work like magic!) that I might dip into the kit and pull out a tool.

In the same way that everything is connected to everything else in the 'quantum soup', all the techniques and tools in this book are connected. In a sense, they are all different facets of the same diamond. The diamond is the essence of the quantum skills and, when describing a particular tool, it is as if we are describing this essence as seen through the filter of that tool. In other words, the tools are all different ways of describing the same thing.

Therefore, for example, Tool Two is the formula E+R=O (the Event + our Response = the Outcome), which helps us to comprehend that we always have a choice in every situation and, in using that choice, we are likely to produce an outcome that will be helpful to us. It is valuable as a stand-alone tool, but another aspect to it is its use in helping us to recognise and manage our emotions when they cloud our thinking. This is connected to Tool Five, the Focusing Technique.

In Part One, I described how the quantum skills for coaches came about. What I did not say, though, was that the reason I am writing about the tools and training coaches to use them is because clients and other coaches asked me to. There I was, happily bumbling along coaching my clients and having a grand time, doing the 'weird stuff' or 'process coaching', as I called it, with no thought of passing it on to others. Then other coaches who heard what I was doing asked me if I would teach them, and various clients suggested that I share it with other coaches.

For a long time I said "No" and had all sorts of good reasons why not. Some of the reasons were around the two questions I asked in Chapter Three about whether this was breaking the rules of coaching and how safe it was to work in this way. I felt that, because I am pretty intuitive, I was probably exercising a lot of safety measures, which I could not describe and would not know how to communicate to others. Also, I did not really want to put myself in the public view by writing a book. However, eventually I came around to accepting that coaching in this way does produce quite amazing results and that many coaches and their clients might benefit from my making it accessible. So here it is.

CHAPTER FOUR

Tool One: visualisation – everything is connected

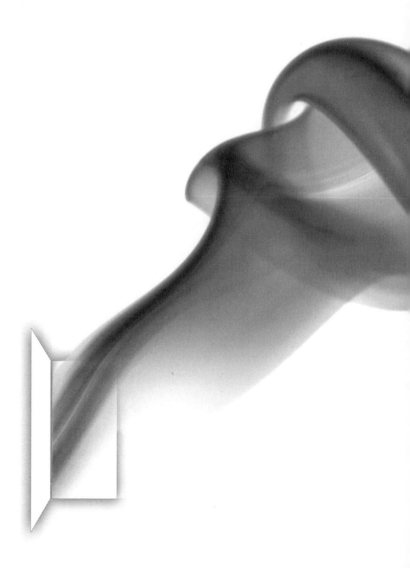

Here is an exercise for you to try for yourself, add to your own personal tool kit and then share with your clients. Ask someone to read out these instructions to you so that you can do it without looking at the page. Do try to resist the temptation to read it first.

- Stand with your feet slightly apart, so you feel well balanced.

- Raise your right arm straight out in front of you at shoulder level as if you are pointing at something but with your index finger pointing upwards.

- Twist your body around to the right, eyes following the tip of your finger. Twist as far as you can and, when you have gone as far as you can comfortably manage (do not strain), note which part of the wall (window or wherever you are facing) your finger is now pointing towards.

- Now gently return back to face the front again.

- Now, you will do this again, but this time in your mind's eye only.

- Think of a baby aged about ten months who you know or have known. Imagine that you are as soft, flexible and bendy as this baby. Shut your eyes and imagine you have raised your arm in front of you as you did just now.

- In your mind's eye only, imagine yourself twisting around as you did just now. You are so soft and flexible that you can go a lot further than you did the first time.

- When you have gone as far as you can, in your mind's eye, return to face the front again.

- You are going to do this once again, still in your mind's eye. This time, though, you are made entirely of rubber, as if you were a bendy toy, like the bendy cowboys or clowns that little children play with.

- Once again, shut your eyes and in your mind's eye raise your arm. Imagine yourself twisting around and around as far as you can. Wow, you are so bendy you can twist all the way round this time – all the way around so that you are now facing the front again! And 'wheeee!', make just another little twist for good luck.

- Now, untwist, uncurl your body and return to the front again. When you are there, open your eyes.

- Try it again, for real this time. Raise your arm and twist your body around as far as you can.

- I know – you are smiling! You probably travelled a lot further than the first time. Yes? I would say between ten and fifteen percent further? So, you have increased your performance in the arm-twisting department by that much, with half a minute's visualisation. Wow! Not bad!

- Now, try it once more, in your mind's eye again. This time, imagine that you are an oak tree – solid and rigid, you have a five foot girth and you are not moving anywhere!

- Shut your eyes and in your mind's eye try to raise your arm. You find this difficult because you are so stiff and rigid. Now try to twist round. You are so solid and inflexible, it really hurts, you really have to strain and you can hardly move. Wow, it really hurts.

- When you have gone as far as you can, untwist and come creaking back to the front again, slowly and painfully. Open your eyes.

- Now, try it again for real. Arm up and twist around as far as you can.

- Hmmm. This time, I think you are smiling a different kind of smile. You probably could not go very far. Perhaps you could not move at all. If you could, it was probably either a lot less than the first time or it was very uncomfortable. Yes?

- So, just in case you thought that the reason you moved further on the second attempt was because, having done it once before, your muscles were limbered up, you are wrong! Now, on the third attempt your muscles are less able than before.

There is quite a lot to think about here.

- If I had asked you to try to push further that first time, you would probably have strained your muscles uncomfortably.

- You saw that, when you saw yourself made of rubber, you were visualising playfully, outrageously, unrealistically and you achieved a good chunk of what you visualised.

- When you imagined yourself as an oak tree, you restricted your vision of what you could achieve and your body, previously very capable, became less able to achieve the task.

- So, what you can achieve is dependant upon how you see yourself performing.

Have you ever used this technique in the past? Perhaps unconsciously? Maybe in playing some form of sport you saw yourself achieving a standard beyond what you usually manage. It is a technique used extensively in the sports arena as well as in healing and in the business world.

Medical studies have shown that when cancer patients visualise their white blood cells as being amoeba gobbling up the cancer cells, or a knight on a charger driving his lance through the cancerous cells, the cancer cell count reduces after the visualisation session. The plethora of books on healing that cram the shelves in today's bookshops describe countless other examples of how healing is brought about through visualising.

When you watch Olympic athletes preparing themselves just prior to an event with their eyes shut in a kind of trance, they are not just 'psyching' themselves up, they are visualising themselves achieving superhuman feats of achievement, clearing the high bar with two feet to spare or running like a gazelle.

There is a classic sports study in which two basketball teams participated in a practice session. One team practised for an hour in the usual way. The other team simply sat and visualised themselves playing like champions and making perfect baskets during this time. After an hour, the two teams played off against each other and the visualising team significantly outplayed their opponents.

Remember, though, this technique is a double-edged sword that can work against you as well as for you. We are all visualising constantly, whether we realise it or not. You order a bowl of spaghetti in an Italian restaurant with a glance at your white shirt. Within seconds after thinking "I mustn't drop any sauce down my front", a dollop has virtually leapt out of the bowl and onto your shirt. As you look at your new car, you are thinking "I will really try not to get a scratch on it" and, hey presto, within two weeks the scratch appears. Whatever you focus on you will get, even if it is what you don't want. The universe is like a vast copying machine: whatever you think about, you order. The universe will just produce it for you as if saying "This is what you ordered!" You may say "No, I didn't order this burglary/losing my job/spraining my ankle" but, if you were focusing on avoiding those things, you have ordered them. You will get what you really really want. You will also get what you really really don't want. So, don't put energy into things you don't believe in.

Energy goes where attention flows

Whatever you project through your thoughts will be delivered straight back to you. When you think about the way something will happen, you have already pre-created or designed it. Making it happen is the automatic next stage, whether or not it is the outcome you really want. When you try to achieve something, you will achieve a chunk of it. When you visualised yourself made of rubber and twisting all the way around, you didn't achieve that in reality, but you did achieve a big chunk of it.

Now try this. Move your chair into the middle of the room to face the window. Imagine that your key objective at work is the equivalent of moving from where you are in the middle of the room to reaching the window – this is where you have to get to in order to get your pay cheque at the end of the month. You see yourself getting there, achieving all that you have to achieve. And of course, as in the arm-twisting exercise, you will achieve a chunk of it. You may perhaps get three quarters of the way from your chair to the window. Not total, glorious success but a good chunk. This is typically how we see ourselves achieving our successes.

If you look outside the window, what is the farthest thing you can see? A tree, a house, a park across the road? Say it's a park, for example. You still need to get to the window to achieve your objective, but this time you tell yourself you are going to get as far as the park, much further than you need to achieve. So you visualise yourself getting there, just as you did when imagining yourself as the bendy toy a moment ago. When you visualise, you are connecting with your inner, natural child – playfully outrageous and unfettered – unconcerned with what is 'realistic'. You think "How can I get there? Well, I could sprout turbo-jets on my heels and zoom over there. Or I could grow springs in my knees and bounce there. Or I could fly like superman wearing my knickers over my tights." And you do it. You visualise yourself getting there.

The next stage is very important. *You imagine yourself being there.* You touch the park bench and feel how it feels to the touch. You look at the world from the vantage point of the park. What can you see around you from that place? You look back at the building you are in now and see how it looks; you even try to look through the window at the chair you are sitting on. Most importantly of all, you feel the feeling of success at having got there. Feel the thrill of your achievement – what this means in your life, the confidence it gives you. Feel this feeling in your body, breathe it in. Enjoy it.

Then, from where you are, still in your chair (this is quite a playful exercise), you will try to get to the park. Of course, once again you will achieve a chunk of it: you won't actually reach the park. You'll probably get halfway between the window and the park. But it is a whole lot further than the window, which is where you need to reach. This is outstanding performance. So, you can produce outstanding performance by visualising yourself achieving far, far more than you need to.

The primary rule for visualising is to *feel the feeling* that you will have when you have achieved the outcome you want. This means that, since you have pre-created the experience of success in your body, you will then behave automatically as if you had already achieved it.

This is one of the natural laws of the universe. It is called the Law of Attraction,[4] and, whether we recognise it as such or not, everything in life will work this way. We might as well recognise this and work with it to get the results we want. This takes us back to wisdom being: understanding the way the world works and working with it to get the results that you want. Our feelings trigger the Law of Attraction, which is equivalent in energetic potency to the Law of Intent. We are all responsible for thinking well and we can choose to do this. In Chapter Seven, I describe another tool that shows how we can learn to make this choice.

Visualisation is a technique that you can have hours of fun playing with. A playful approach is highly recommended. You can start by visualising small things like parking spaces. It is

---

4. The film *The Secret* gives a memorable rendering of how the Law of Attraction operates.

amazing how often this works. You are driving into town on a Saturday morning and, instead of thinking "I'll never find anywhere to park", you see yourself entering the car park and, as you do so, a red car pulls out of a space to your left and you drive into it. Sometimes, you might find it is a white car and it vacates a space on the right! But hey, who's arguing? You can also put it to some serious use – improving your presentation skills, preparing yourself mentally for a job interview or buying the house of your dreams.

Presenting this tool to your clients

When you feel that you have got a good handle on using this tool and are experiencing the amazing results it produces in your life, this is the time to introduce it to your clients. You can lead them through the arm-swinging exercise in exactly the same way as I described it to you and debrief the exercise with the same learning points as I gave to you. (You can usefully repeat to your client everything I wrote after the line "There is quite a lot to think about here", which comes immediately after the exercise.) This is also a good moment to describe the 'quantum soup theory', which I covered in Chapter One, using more or less the same kind of words as I did. I have reproduced the relevant paragraphs below as a reference.

"Quantum theory says that everything that exists is made up of tiny parcels of energy vibrating at different frequencies. The more solid a thing appears to be, the slower its vibration; the less solid it appears, the faster or finer the vibration.

"So, the particles that make up a solid, wooden table have a fairly slow frequency compared to, say, your body, which, being a little less solid than the table, has a finer vibration. And absolutely everything that exists, is made up of energy vibrating like this. We already know, for example, that sound is a vibration; we have much technology that

works on this basis and is able to measure this vibration. Colour is also a vibration – the difference between colours is simply a difference in frequency – and crystals have a unique kind of frequency.

"The space between objects is also energy vibrating very rapidly. In fact, there really is no space and there really are no objects. The whole universe is a kind of 'energy soup' with bits floating around in it all resonating at different frequencies. Those bits look like separate objects to us but they are really just the place where the soup is a bit thicker.

"So, we have seen that thoughts are a fine and yet powerful form of energetic vibration. People often tend to think of thoughts as being insubstantial. We say 'It's only a thought' as if it is less significant than something more tangible, like an event. This is not the case: a thought can have as much impact on our life as an event and, in fact, may be a critical factor in creating that event. Most quantum physicists agree that when we think a thought, some key things happen. The first is that the thought, which has properties similar to a magnet (because we are essentially electromagnetic beings), shimmers out into the energy soup and connects with other things in the soup that resonate with it. In other words, it attracts things, such as events, that are similar to it. This, very simply put, is how we create the events in our lives.

"Another key thing that happens when we think a thought, according to the quantum physicists, is that, as well as shimmering out into, and becoming a part of, the energy soup, the thought swims into the energy that is our own body. In the same way that plugging an electrical appliance into a wall socket connects it to the electricity supply allowing the current to flow, our thought connects with every part of our body. It actually flows into the molecules of our body, into the cells and eventually if we

think a particular kind of thought often enough into our DNA. So, in essence, we become what we think."

This then, is a useful way to introduce the client to the concept of the Law of Attraction, which is a key tool in the tool kit. Many of the other tools support or further illustrate this, which takes us back to the 'different facets of the same diamond' idea.

Here are the key points to cover as you present Tool One, visualisation, to your clients.

- We achieve a chunk of what we visualise.
- What we can achieve is dependant upon how we see ourselves performing: it is a double-edged sword and can work for us or against us.
- The universe is like a vast copying machine: what we visualise, we order and the universe presents it to us. *Energy flows where attention goes.*
- The key is to feel the feeling that you will feel when you achieve what you want. Feelings trigger the Law of Attraction, which is equivalent in energetic potency to the Law of Intent.
- Be playful, unfettered, outrageous and light-hearted in your visualisation and use it in all life situations.

And remember, before introducing Tool One to your clients make it a part of your own life.

CHAPTER FIVE

Our emotions

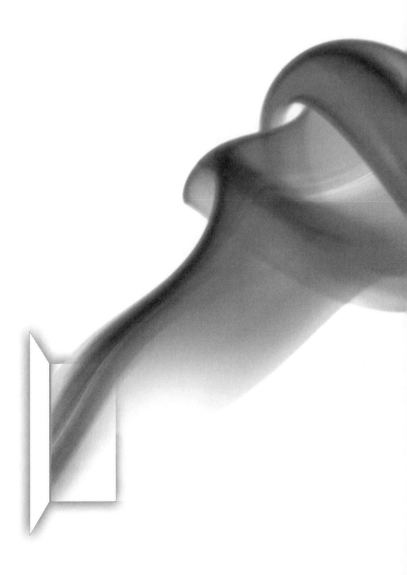

What is an emotion?

Before we delve into what our emotions are about, let's talk a little about the difference between emotions and feelings. Many people see these two words as synonymous and there may not, in fact, be a difference upon which all agree. Sometimes I may also use them synonymously in a context where the difference is not very important. However, the difference between them that I recognise is that an emotion is the body's response to a thought (Tolle, 2005). (This is just my view, of course, it is not cast in stone.)

When we think a thought, we are internally interpreting a situation (which can be current, past or future) and the emotion tells us whether this is something that, for example, we want, like, fear, desire or distrust. It does this through two mediums. One is through the generation of another thought, such as "this is appalling", and the other is through the generation of a physical sensation or feeling, which might be a lurching in the stomach, a tingling in the chest, a certain lightness in the head and so on. A feeling is, then, the physical experience of an emotion, which in turn is the body's response to a thought.

Some areas of psychology and therapy state that the emotion comes first and the thought follows, and I will not argue this point dogmatically. However, where we stand on this question may depend on how we define a thought. Thoughts do not always appear in the laborious form of words. Sometimes the content of the thought, i.e. the way we are internally interpreting a situation, takes the form of an instantaneous flash of an idea. This may be so rapid that it can feel as if the emotion that is then generated by this thought-flash actually precedes it.

However, having made this differentiation between an emotion and a feeling, I do not adhere rigidly to it. This is because in some instances the two are linked and sometimes it just sounds odd to say 'emotion' rather than 'feeling'. For example, in the next sentence when I refer to feelings, I am really talking about emotions leading to physical sensations: in other words, both emotions and feelings.

In the visualisation exercise, we saw that the primary rule in visualising or pre-creating what you want to achieve is to feel the feeling that you will have when you have achieved it. So, you behave as if you have already achieved it.

Feelings, then, are the key to manifesting your reality. *Feelings are the key*. Full stop. They are the key to fully living and fully being alive. We will spend some time now looking at the role that our feelings and emotions play in our lives.

The reason for having emotions

All of our physiological functions stem from a biological reason to do with nourishment, physical survival or reproduction. Why do we yawn? The most plausible explanation, and the one that is taught in medical school, is that we yawn because oxygen levels in our lungs are low. Why does our digestive system shut down in an emergency? Because all our energy and resources are needed in our muscles, which are about to be exerted in the fight or flight response, and digestion would use up some of this valuable energy. Why do we sweat? This is our body's way of cooling itself, whether that extra heat comes from hardworking muscles or from overstimulated nerves. Why do certain muscles develop when we exercise? Because the body is very economical and only develops those muscles that are used regularly. Muscles that are underused are not given the same nutrients for growth. Why do we feel physical pain? To alert us to the fact that something is wrong and to instruct us to attend to it. If we didn't treat a wound, it might get infected, become gangrenous and result in the loss of a limb.

Why, then, do we suffer emotional pain? For much the same reason as we suffer physical pain: to tell us that something is wrong. *Pay attention!* This is the purpose of our emotions. Emotions are like a red flag to tell us to pay attention to something, not to tell us to respond in a particular way or in an unconscious, knee-jerk fashion. Emotions are good signposts but poor navigators. They act as pointers and provide information about what is going on for us but they don't tell us what to do. Most of us do not realise this and we tend to react to emotions rather than listen to them.

We can learn so much about what is going on for us by learning to observe and listen to the information that our bodies give us through our emotions. When we deepen our ability to listen to our bodies we learn to pick up the signs that we're having an emotion and then we can decide what we need to do about it. This means we have to learn to be aware of how an emotion feels – to be aware of the subtle physical sensation of the emotion happening in our body.

Tool Two: the awareness muscle

Most of us just don't pay attention to the physical sensation that is generated in our body through an emotion. So if our ability to be aware of these feelings in our body were a muscle, in most people it would be pretty flabby through underuse. As we saw above, our body does not send as many nutrients to underused parts of itself, which consequently do not develop in the same way as muscles that are frequently exercised.

You may feel a surge of panic welling up when you see a former boss who constantly bullied you, walking towards you along the street. You instantly start thinking about how you can protect yourself. "Shall I cross the street? Shall I scowl at him or ignore him?" You are trying to work out how you can move away from the discomfort or emotional pain and move towards pleasure. This drive away from pain and towards pleasure is a fundamental human response to unwelcome situations. So, you ignore the message that your body is giving through the welling up and surging sensation and go straight to the brain for a solution. You are treating the emotion simply as a trigger for an action rather than a source of information. Your brain, splendid organ though it may be, is very limited. It is limited by what makes sense to it, what is logical. This may be a pretty distorted logic based on what has happened in the past and might therefore happen in the future. In fact, when we engage the brain in this way during an emotional experience, in taking us back to the miserable past or projecting into the scary future, it produces secondary emotions, guilt or anxiety, for example, that compound the whole experience even further.

So, you are feeling this surging, welling panic in your gut as you remember how beastly your boss was to you, and the thoughts come rushing in. You feel a great stab of anger as you recall one particular humiliation and then a gust of throbbing anger with yourself for having allowed it. This is followed by a torrent of guilt that you didn't have enough self-esteem to tell him what a bully he was. And, suddenly, you are overcome with a tidal wave of depression making you feel weak and helpless in the face of it all. Or perhaps, as he walks towards you, you decide to tell him how miserable he made your life at that time. The thought of doing this is satisfying, after all he is no longer your boss, but now you feel waves of nauseous anxiety gripping your stomach, as you fear how he might lash out at you.

The initial feeling that hit you was pain. Emotional pain. Pure and simple. Then, as your brain fired off and took you into the past, you were blasted by several secondary emotions: anger against him, self-anger, guilt and finally depression. The anxiety about the future scenario of challenging him was also a secondary emotion.

With each new secondary emotion, you are getting a raft of new thoughts to explain and interpret the feeling, and you are getting further and further away from the initial sense of pain.

This trip through the gamut of negative emotions is all in the vain attempt to move away from pain and towards pleasure. When we learn to experience pain in the present moment, feeling safe in the innate ability of our body to handle it, we can reduce the time we spend there and the impact it has upon us. This is what happened to me as I climbed down into my 'well of pain' all those years ago. Pain itself is not dangerous, but the anger, self-anger, guilt, depression and anxiety can well and truly impede our mental wellbeing.

To develop your awareness muscle is to pay attention to all the feelings that you would not normally pay attention to – with your brain disengaged, so the flow of thoughts is stemmed. Since a thought generates an emotion, stemming the flow of thoughts prevents additional emotions from kicking in and adding yet another layer of emotion.

This is a tool that I give to all my clients and many of them find it very difficult. Some say week after week "I still can't get this awareness muscle thing" and I always reply "Keep on at it, you'll suddenly get what it's about." And eventually they do. The more you do this, the stronger the so-called 'muscle' becomes and the easier it is to do it. Same as working out in the gym really!

Try it now. Think of something that is making you feel a little anxious at the moment. Not the great big thing that is scaring the wits out of you; something that is causing a minor perturbation in your natural serenity. Say to yourself (out loud if you are alone) "I really can't handle this." Where do you feel this in your body? How does it feel? Describe the sensation to yourself. Now think of the same thing again and say to yourself "I can easily handle this. It's a breeze." How does it feel this time? Describe the feeling in your body.

You probably felt sensations of energy sinking or flowing out of you or heaviness in your gut the first time. And when you said "I can handle this", I suspect it felt a lot lighter, flowing upwards, outwards or expanding – something like that or variations on those themes. This exercise has given you an example of noticing feeling sensations in your body and is a tool that you can use for yourself and share with your clients.

These are the steps that I suggest you follow to develop your awareness muscle, at any time during the day when you begin to sense an emotion coming into play within you, such as anxiety, frustration, elation, irritation, pleasure or grumpiness.

1. Just register that "I am feeling an emotion right now."
2. Focus on exactly what you are feeling in your body and where you are feeling it. Is it in your head, your shoulders, your limbs, your chest, solar-plexus, stomach? What does it feel like? Is it moving? If so, where – upwards, downwards? Is it surging like waves or zipping like electricity? Is it spiky or smooth? What colour is it?
3. Remember how these emotions feel; jot them down if you can. Treat this like a scientific survey of yourself. Study yourself and take a real interest in the information your body is generating.

Here's another exercise that I usually ask clients to try. Do it now. Hold up a hand in front of you and, with your eyes closed, focus on it and sense how you would know that your hand is still there now that you can't see it. Can you sense the 'feeling of hand'? Perhaps it is like a tingling to start with then becomes a general feeling of aliveness. Now extend this awareness to your other hand and to your arms and then to your whole body. Feel how alive your body is.

This is 'being present in your body' and takes you totally into the moment. You cannot be anywhere else when you are present within your body and alert in this way. It is incredibly beneficial for your health to do this and is simultaneously energising and relaxing. I would encourage you to 'go into your body' in this way as often during the day as you can. If you remember to be present in your body at odd moments, especially when you are feeling uptight, anxious, glazed over or anything other than feeling great, you will enhance your day enormously.

Fast and slow feelings

Recent research has shown that there are two different kinds of feelings. The first are 'slow': essential, still, soul feelings of peace, bliss, acceptance, stillness, love, silence and even sadness. (Sadness is not the same as unhappiness or feeling sorry for yourself.) The other feelings of anger, aggression, jealousy and rage can be called 'fast' feelings, which arise from our primitive heritage. If you are suddenly overwhelmed by fear or anger, the fight or flight mechanism kicks in, producing a rush of adrenalin that lasts physiologically for three minutes, plus or minus a few seconds. If you are within snarling distance of a lion, you need these three minutes of adrenalin rush to act fast, giving you the energy to get away or be gotten. After three minutes, it is over.

This biological response mechanism still continues to operate within us now, and has done throughout our evolution. There is nothing wrong with these feelings; they are a perfectly natural part of our functioning, as long as we let them go after the three-minute deadline. However, if we continue to feel a 'fast feeling' after this period, it becomes not a release but something psychological. We get stuck into it and have a strong desire to hang onto it. Then we crank up the feelings by going into the "What's more, I remember what else you did" mode, which is an example of a thought creating an emotion. This causes our serotonin levels to decrease by more than 30% and it takes six hours to replenish our energy levels.

But, if we can let that feeling go and not hang onto it after the three minutes, *the fast feeling automatically changes into a slow feeling*. We are often told to control our emotions and that it is wrong to be angry, jealous, fearful and so on, but these feelings are a biological evolutionary necessity. What we need to do is feel it for three minutes only and then let it go. When we have a slow feeling, we get a tremendous increase in serotonin, which gives us a feel-good moment. Feeling good automatically produces serotonin, thus creating a virtuous circle.

Of course, it is easier to *talk about* letting the fast feeling go than to *do it*. Acquiring this ability is a crucial life skill and, once we learn it, it changes our lives. The awareness muscle is a key player here, and I will show you how in Chapter Eight when we look at a technique called focusing, which is our Tool Five.

Using the awareness muscle to manage our emotions by letting go of fast feelings is the essence of what is called 'emotional intelligence', which we will look at next.

CHAPTER SIX

Working with our emotions

The limbic brain

In the field of research into what is called 'emotional intelligence', some fascinating data has been uncovered. All the books that I recommend in this chapter are really essential reading for anyone interested in using these quantum skills, particularly Daniel Goleman's book, *Emotional Intelligence*, which gives a wealth of information about the link between our brain and our emotions. To put it very simply, this is a summary of Goleman's explanation of the structure of the 'emotional brain'. I often recount this to clients, as it is immensely valuable for them to have an understanding of this aspect of their make-up.

The limbic brain is an ancient part of the brain in evolutionary terms and is situated at the base of the skull. It is the emotional centre of the brain. At the heart of the limbic brain sits an almond-shaped structure called the amygdala. As we interact with the world in our day-to-day lives, all the information that we gather through the use of our five senses is channelled, via an array of neurons, through the amygdala to the frontal cortex of the brain, which is where we do all our cognitive, logical thinking.

In *Emotional Intelligence*, Goleman tells the story of a highly successful lawyer who underwent surgery to have a tumour removed from his brain. Although the surgery was a success, his life changed dramatically afterwards. He lost his job and was unable to hold down any other jobs. His wife left him and, after making a series of poor investment decisions he lost his house and had to resort to living with a family member. Extensive intellectual tests showed that his mental faculties were unimpaired but, nevertheless, he went to see a neurologist to see if they could throw any light on the mystery.

When, at the end of the first session, the neurologist asked him to choose a date for a second meeting, the patient was thrown into a turmoil of indecision. He could find reasons for and against every date and time the neurologist suggested but he could not choose one of them. He had no sense of how he felt about any of these dates and so, without this awareness, he had no preference at all. This gave the doctor the clue that during the operation the neural links between the limbic brain and the frontal cortex had been damaged.

One lesson that the neurologist, Dr Antonio Damasio, learned from this, and which has been confirmed through extensive studies of similar patients, is that feelings play a crucial role in decision making. All of our decisions, be they minor ones such as whether to go for a walk or not, or major decisions such as who to marry, where to send the kids to school or how to direct our career, have an emotional component to them.

We all make many decisions every day. In organisations, decision making is the name of the game. Unless we are able to recognise that emotions are driving us as we choose one decision over another and that others are making decisions in the same emotion-driven way, we are missing out on vital information that we could use to improve the outcomes we create. As a leadership coach, I make this point over and over to my clients. Leadership is essentially *getting results through others*. To get great results from others, a leader needs to understand what the individuals in their team need in order to perform well. So there is a strong business case for recognising the crucial role people's emotions play in their day-to-day functioning.

Mirror neurons

Here is one version of an experiment, the essence of which has been conducted dozens of times in a variety of similar ways. It shows how emotions can be transmitted from one person to another through the quantum soup in a direct way, which can seem to be almost virus-like.

Two people are sitting silently in a room together. One is in a state of high emotional arousal, either very angry or very joyful; the other, at that moment, is in a rather more bland emotional state, not feeling anything very strongly. After ten or fifteen minutes, the experiment shows that the person with the blander emotional level has 'caught' the other's more powerful emotion. We hardly need a scientific experiment to point this out to us: we all know how true it is. How contagious other people's emotions are and how easy it is to catch them! Again this is something that we all, as human beings, need to take onboard in our interactions with others, and, as a coach, it is a tremendously valuable concept to help your clients to fully appreciate. In the workplace, if a person is feeling irritated, anxious or frustrated as they go into a meeting, they can be certain that the others in the room will catch this within a very short time and thus contaminate the effectiveness of the meeting. We are all far more responsible for the way events unfold around us than we often realise.

I said above that this is due to the emotions being transmitted through the quantum soup, but we could also offer a more physiological explanation and say that this phenomenon is due to the function of mirror neurons. A mirror neuron is a nerve cell that fires both when a person (or an animal) performs an action, as well as when they observe this action being performed by another. Thus, the neuron mirrors the behaviour of the other person exactly as though the observer were performing the action. So, for example, if football supporters are fully immersed in watching a football match, the neurons will cause their muscles to fire off in exactly the same way as if they were playing the game themselves. Therapists working with anorexic people often begin to feel hungry during a therapy session. People seeing someone yawn often start yawning themselves. I remember how a school friend and I used to start a 'class yawn' every week in one of our lessons. For fun, we would each simulate a yawn during the lesson and within five minutes the whole class would be yawning!

Serotonin

Doc Childre and Howard Martin in their book *The HeartMath Solution* provide many examples of experiments and research into the effect of the heart's activities upon the mind and body. Among these is an experiment, similar to the one described above, in which a dozen or so people in a room are connected to monitors that measure the serotonin level in their bodies. When one person in the room, unbeknown to the others, goes 'into their feelings' allowing them to feel their heart relaxing and opening, this increases their serotonin levels by 30%. An amazing knock-on effect of this is that the serotonin level of all the other people in the room also increases, even though they do not know that the one person is doing this. Wow!

The implications of this for us all and for you as a coach are immense. You can show your clients that when they go into their hearts during a tense meeting, for example, it will change the energy in the room, increasing others' feel-good factor and thus their performance. This research has shown that the higher-concentration energy generally affects the lower-concentration energy around it. This is why the person with the strong feelings, in a state of high emotional arousal, influenced the person with the 'bland' feelings in the earlier experiment. This tendency is called entrainment, which is the tendency for two oscillating bodies to lock into phase so that they vibrate in harmony. And, of course, the implications for you as a coach are also significant. You are having an effect upon your client as you sit with them and you can raise their serotonin levels and enhance the impact of their coaching experience.

The body produces around seven different types of serotonin. Most people think that all hormones are produced in the brain but there are many studies showing that certain hormones, including one called serotonin B, are produced and manufactured in the physiological heart. This does not mean that the heart is a gland but that it acts like a brain. *The HeartMath Solution* gives extensive examples of, and techniques to work with, what they call the brain-in-the-heart, the heart's own independent and very complex nervous system discovered by neuroscientists Amour and Ardell. Their premise is that the heart has an intelligence – a mind, which influences the emotions and perceptions. Hormone testing shows that when serotonin B is produced in the heart it travels to the brain and into the centre behind the cortex, which governs social function – the ability of humans to interact with others. Serotonin B is the only type of serotonin that will go to this centre in the brain. Therefore, the findings indicate that there is a major link between serotonin and our own ability to communicate and interact easily with others. People who suffer from depression are often those whose sensor in the cortex to do with social functioning is not fully operational because physiologically their heart is restricted and is not producing serotonin B.

How does the heart produce serotonin B? This is the lovely part of the story where a whole range of emotional and psychological elements are introduced. When the heart is open emotionally and we are feeling the wonderful slow feelings of wellbeing, we produce serotonin B. Studies show that if a group of people together in a room with a depressive person feel lots of love and compassion for that person it does not necessarily result in that person producing more serotonin B. It is only when the depressed person starts to feel the feelings in their own heart and the energy starts to move that they can then produce the hormone for themselves.

Synchrony and serotonin

Another experiment along the same lines has been conducted under clinical, scientific conditions dozens of times. A group of people in a room is asked to meditate, doing whatever it is that this word means to them. Of course, they may all have entirely different interpretations of the word. They are all hooked up to equipment measuring brainwaves and hormone levels while they are meditating and, again, one person without the others knowing is given the instruction to go into their feelings – to go into their heart and acknowledge what is there and feel their feelings. That person's brainwaves go into a deeper alpha state and, without anything being suggested at all, all the others' brainwaves follow the pattern of that person. In fact, each time this experiment was conducted, after about seven or eight minutes the brainwaves of each person in the room followed suit and synchronised and harmonised with each other and began operating 'as one'.

This kind of research confirms the quantum nature of everything, that we are all connected at every level. So that clients learn from their own experiences (and not just because you tell them so), it is vital for coaches to impart this information to their clients, through:

- Telling them about the research and describing the quantum theories
- Giving them exercises that demonstrate it, either:
  - in the coaching sessions themselves, or
  - for 'homework'.

Of course, as a coach you are already very aware that people operate from different thinking styles and need their coach to work with them in a way that matches their particular way of evaluating information and learning from it. Like many other coaches, in my coaching practice I use the Myers Briggs Type Indicator (MBTI) to gain an understanding of my clients' thinking styles. I also teach it to all those clients who are in a leadership role, as I think it is a tremendously valuable tool for all managers and leaders to use. However, it is not my purpose to describe MBTI here. If you are interested in finding out more about Myers Briggs, information about it is readily available on the internet.

CHAPTER SEVEN

Choice is the most powerful tool we have

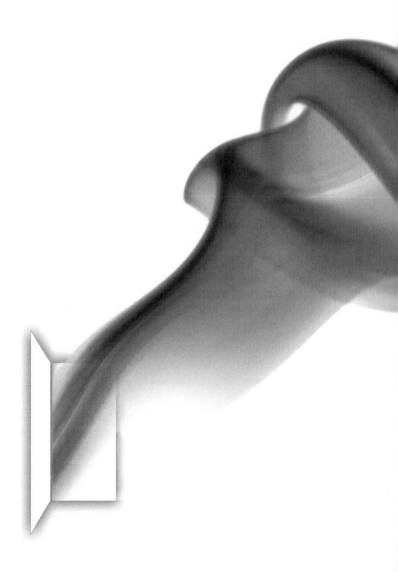

Tool Three: E+R=O

E+R=O is a useful little formula that works in every situation in our lives and is a reminder of how the choices we make affect what happens to us. It is a formula that I have been passing on to others for many years and a number of my clients tell me that it has changed their lives. It is a simple and intuitive truth about which people say "I always knew that!" Nevertheless, until they encounter it in this form, they become aware that they have not applied it mindfully to life's challenges. When they do, it makes an immediate and startling difference to their lives. I know people who make it their screen saver and others who emblazon it on the whiteboard in their office as a reminder of its potency.

It goes like this:

E (the Event) + R (our Response) = O (the Outcome)

Say, for example, your boss comes up to you with a disconcerted frown, asking "Could I have a word with you, now?", this is the Event.

What are you thinking right now, how do you feel and how does this make you respond? The likelihood is that you are going to think something along the lines of "Uh oh! Bad news a-coming", and feel anxious, panicky even (especially if you have been working a little under par lately or have taken a couple of days sick leave for a not-so-valid reason.) So, you may present yourself in your boss's office a little on the defensive side and less than open to really listening to what her concerns may be. It turns out that she is concerned about the ability of Martin, the newcomer to your team, and wondering if he is just having difficulty in settling in or whether she made a mistake in hiring him. Because you are ready to hear something negative about your own performance, somehow you read this as a subtle dig at your managerial capabilities and you fire off a sarcastic comment at a particularly inappropriate moment. (This is the Response.)

What happens next? Maybe your boss, who was genuinely trying to seek your views on the problem, will feel that you think she is being judgemental or unduly demanding of a newcomer and will be reluctant to express similar views to you in future. Maybe . . . well, fill in the blank yourself. There are half a dozen alternative scenarios, which reflect that your relationship has taken a hit. (This is the Outcome.)

Then what? When a relationship starts to deteriorate, it can affect everything in its path, but this could signal a steady downward spiral contaminating any future problem-solving situations between the two of you. Six months later, you feel mightily aggrieved when your boss does not recommend you for the next promotion in your grade.

Let's consider an alternative to the original Event (your boss asks to have a word with you). After the initial thought of "Uh oh! Bad news a-coming", although you feel somewhat apprehensive about your recent performance and attendance, you decide that, if your boss challenges you on this, you will admit that you have been a little unfocused of late and will address the problem. Having made this decision, you feel a little calmer and are able to listen to what your boss says without your emotions getting in the way. When she confides to you her concerns about Martin, you sense her worry and let her know that Martin is having some challenges at home, which he is dealing with. You add that he is basically thorough and competent and this will become more evident when he has sorted out his private life.

As a result of this conversation, your boss feels that she can speak to you in confidence and over the next few months your relationship becomes more solid. And, of course, when the promotion vacancy arises . . .

Choice is the most powerful tool we have in our kit – as we *always, always have a choice over how we respond to any situation*. Even when we feel we have no choice at all, we can press the 'pause button' and consider what we want our outcome to be and what response is most likely to lead to it. A few years ago, I came across a quotation by Viktor Frankl (holocaust survivor and famous author and psychoanalyst), which encapsulates E+R=O:

> *"Between stimulus and response there is a space. In this space lies our freedom to choose our response. In those choices lie our growth and our happiness."*

Whenever clients describe something that has just happened and which clearly illustrates the lessons in E+R=O, I will generally make a note to share the formula with them. If it is not appropriate to do this at the time, because there are more important avenues to explore, I will make a note to talk about it at another time, linking it back to the incident mentioned. There are several interesting points about E+R=O, which I describe to clients.

- **The Response has three contiguous components:** one leading to the next, often within the space of a nano-second. The Thinking Response kicks in instantly, followed by the Feeling Response as an emotion of some sort takes over, leading us to the Actioned Response as we actually do or say something in response to the Event. The usual question of whether thought or emotion comes first can be asked here and there are a variety of answers, all of which are interesting. My sense is that, as human beings with a non-stop flow of thoughts streaming through our minds, it is probably a thought of some kind that comes first, but not necessarily in the form of words. Sometimes a thought can appear as a kind of flash of perceived knowing, and I think that an emotion is our body's response to a thought. However, the argument about this can rage on for hours and ultimately it does not really matter very much as long as we learn something about how not to let this take control of us. What is fairly certain, though, is that emotions do lead to actions or behaviours, so the sequence of Thinking Response–Emotional Response–Actioned Response does make some sense. The important thing is that we can work with this to help us manage our emotions more effectively and choose our action, i.e. the final of the three Response components. It is in working with this tripartite response tendency, to which human beings are innately subject, that quantum skills for coaches display their similarity to cognitive behaviour therapy. You might remember that, when I touched on this in an earlier chapter, I showed how CBT recognises the same response pattern firing off from thought to action.

■ **The Outcome becomes a new Event in our lives** to which we then have to choose a new Response. If we choose a Response that aggravates the situation, for example, your boss snaps back at your sarcastic reply (new Event) and you say to your boss that she is always unreasonably critical (new Response), the spiral continues all the way downward to the lack of promotion six months later.

So, this means that we are actually creating the events in our lives on a moment-by-moment basis. In fact, every time we respond to anyone about anything we are creating an event. An actioned response can be anything from a verbal comment to a facial expression or physical gesture or a mere raising of an eyebrow or looking heavenwards. Something as minor as this can set in motion a downward spiral of events that will have repercussions months later. And that is just the actioned response, of course. Even though the preceding stages of thought and emotional response may only occur a nano-second or so beforehand, the other people involved in the event are also experiencing them. How? Through the quantum soup!

The energetic vibration of both the thought and the emotion will communicate their essence to all involved.

We all know people who always seem to have good luck. Nauseating, isn't it? But when we understand that they are actually creating these pleasant happenstances by continually choosing helpful responses to all kinds of situations whether or not these situations are desired, it does not seem quite so unfathomable. I was only joking about it being nauseating; it is actually pretty cool.

It is very easy to choose to be considerate, to listen attentively, to see the other person's point of view when we are happy with what is happening and it does not produce any emotion of anxiety, frustration, irritation or downright anger. It is a whole lot more difficult when we are experiencing any of these emotions and, just for that moment (even though we know that the 'right thing' to do is to listen, see the other person's viewpoint and so on), we just don't feel like it. Full stop. Any smarty-pants who suggests to us that we might benefit from counting to ten before reacting gets the full weight of our most lethal sneer. But it is just when we do feel these incapacitating emotions that we will benefit the most from applying this formula. Of course, we know this, but how do we do it when our emotions are running the show? We will explore this in depth throughout the rest of the book.

- **The time lag between Response and Outcome can be anything from instantaneous to years later.** We often don't know the extent to which something pleasant or unpleasant that happens to us has been created by a Response we made sometime in the past.

In the situation with the boss, your sarcastic comment produces an immediate hostile retort so it is easy to see the Outcome as it happens. It may be that the Outcome does not happen until the following day, or the following week or month or year. Say, for example you are at a conference and you meet someone who wants to tell you his life story during a coffee break and you just listen because he obviously needs to dump his feelings onto a stranger at that moment. You think nothing more of it. He, however, has never experienced being really listened to in that way and it impresses him greatly.

Two years later when he has started his own business, which is growing like crazy, and is looking for someone to head up his sales department, he then remembers "There was that guy I met at that conference back in 2008 who was a brilliant listener. He's just the person I need." And he rummages around to find your business card, calls you out of the blue and offers you the job. Luck or what? Things really do happen in this way and, when you start to choose more mindful responses to the events in your life, you will find that 'luck' starts to happen more and more often. Little moments of serendipity seem to emerge from nowhere and you can't always pin them down as being the result of this or that action, but life just starts to get sweeter.

■ Even if this seems like a very obvious process, when we truly take it onboard and become more mindful, more conscious, about how we react to events, it has the potential to change the way we experience our lives. It is pretty crucial that, before you talk about this to your clients, you consciously build it into your own life and experience the shifts that it brings about as you develop the habit of making conscious choices. Then, as you work with your clients, make sure that at some point quite early in the coaching programme you describe it to them. After that, it becomes the reference point to return to when they talk about things that have not worked out.

You can help your clients to apply the formula by describing the following step-by-step process.

1. When an event occurs that you don't like and you feel is about to catapult you into a worse situation, STOP!

2. Remember: *between stimulus and response there is a space. In this space lies our freedom to choose our response. In those choices lie our growth and our happiness.* The space may only be a fraction of a second long but once you have accessed it you can sit in that space for as long as you need, freeze the frame and ask these two questions:

a) Outcome setting – "What would I like to happen as a result of this Event?" or "What Outcome do I want to achieve here?" This should be an Outcome that will be for the good of all involved.

b) Response to achieve that Outcome – "What do I have to do to make this happen?"

Question a) is the most important in a way and there are two aspects to choosing the Outcome that we want, which are:

i) What do we want to happen in a practical, logistic, material sense? For example, we want:

■ a colleague to agree to the solution or course of action we have proposed

■ our boss/team/client to recognise our contribution to the project

■ to be given the promotion/opportunity to test a new skill/lead on a phase of a project

ii) How do we want the other person or people in the situation to feel, either about us or about the Outcome described above. Many people when using E+R=O tend to focus only on the first aspect, which can lead them to drive their own agenda forward regardless of how others feel about it or about them. Remember, when you are interacting with another person they are having an experience of you. People will always forget what you said. People will always forget what you did. But people will never forget how you made them feel. If their experience of you leads them to feel ignored, disenfranchised, put down, frustrated or demeaned, this

will play itself out in the new Event that will be created
and will not serve you

3. Act on whatever it is that you have identified in step 2.
Coaching is all about action. Nobody ever got wet by
saying the word 'water'. Ultimately, you are encouraging
your clients to do things differently to get different
results in their lives. E+R=O helps them to do this.

The difficulty comes when the situation triggers a strong
emotional response in the client and it is nigh on impossible
for them to get to the place where they want to ask the two
questions: "What Outcome do I want to achieve?" and "What
do I have to do to make this happen?" I address this more
fully in the next chapter, when we look at dealing with
emotions, and throughout the remainder of the book.

CHAPTER EIGHT

Managing our emotions

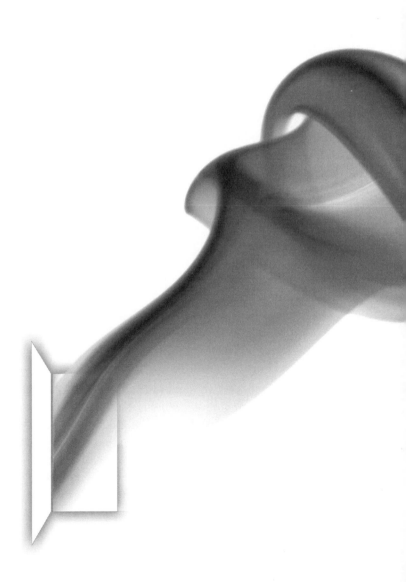

The central ideas that we have looked at so far are: the interconnectedness of all things, the purpose of our emotions, the concept of the awareness muscle and the implications on our lives of using the E+R=O formula. Now we will explore how they all tie in together.

As I said earlier, unless you incorporate all these tools into your own life you cannot convey them to your client with any sense of conviction. I will, therefore, talk about how we can all manage our emotions, rather than just how you can help your client to do this. Everything I say here, though, is material that you can also share with your coaching clients.

Gaining control over your physiology

We left Chapter Seven with an undesirable Event that is producing a whole heap of swirling emotions in you and making you feel like you want to kick the cat. Therefore, you are just not in the mood to remind yourself that E+R will *always* result in O. The old fight or flight mechanism has taken over, adrenalin is running the show and you can feel yourself going along with whatever the emotion drives you to do. What *should* you do?

"Breathe."

"What? Breathe?"

"Yes, breathe! Slowly and from deep within you."

Tool Four: deep breathing

Well, actually, there are two significant things you can do. Deep breathing is one and is probably quite familiar to you but I will mention it anyway in case you do not already use it. When the fight or flight response kicks in, a lot of things happen automatically within the body that enable you to either run or fight, as we saw in Chapter Five. There is a biological need for rapid, shallower breathing (to increase oxygen intake); increased heart and pulse rate (to get oxygen to the vital organs more quickly); tunnel vision (for better visual focus); and shutting down of the digestive system (to minimise unnecessary use of energy). As all these physical activities are totally automatic, we do not have any control over them – well, almost no control. The only area over which we do have some control is our breathing, unless you are a yogic master who can control his own pulse rate. But for the rest of us mere mortals, our breathing is the only part of this response pattern that we can influence.

Remember that, since every part of the body is interconnected, this physiological experience happens as a result of an emotional response to the external Event in your life. So the mind and body are connected. Likewise, all the different elements of this fight or flight response are connected. If you can influence one element of it, all the others will be similarly influenced. When you slow down the rapid, shallow breathing, the heart and pulse rate also slow down, the digestive system kicks back into action and the tunnel vision expands outwards. This, in brief, is how deep breathing works. This is how to demonstrate it to others. Try it now. Put one hand on your chest and one on your stomach. Take a deep breath. Which hand moves the most? You may find the top one moves more. If so, this is not the kind of deep breathing we are talking about. This is deep breathing from your chest, the kind that you find on the parade ground when the sergeant major bellows "Chest out!"

The deep breathing we are interested in is more accurately called 'slow breathing' and comes from deep within you. You can tell if you are doing it if the hand on your stomach moves more than the one on your chest. It feels as if your stomach is gently pushing your hand outwards, rather like the soft breathing of a sleeping baby. Your stomach is pushing your hand out because the diaphragm (the rubber-like sheet below your lungs) is pushing downwards as your lungs expand. Try this now. As you breathe like this, slowly from deep inside of you, find yourself feeling relaxed and calm in your body and in your head and you can probably sense the beating of your heart softly within your chest. This is a really marvellous way of calming your emotions and clearing your head when things go awry. It creates the space in which you are moved to implement E+R=O by asking those two key questions – about identifying the outcome you want and what you have to do to create it.

There are two ways in which you can use this deep breathing technique:

■ **In a crisis** when you need to take control of your emotions in the way described above (this will take a minute or so).

■ **As a daily routine,** by sitting quietly breathing slowly from your abdomen for ten minutes a day (preferably in the morning but evening is good too – both if you are feeling enthusiastic).

Let's look at this second technique in more detail. It has the effect of focusing your attention on the activity of breathing, which we are normally unaware of. This is amazingly beneficial to our systems, physically and mentally, and is one of the most powerful things you can do for yourself. When in this mode, you are putting your brain into an alpha brain state, which is a very regenerating place for it to be.

As you breath from your lower abdomen, you may say to yourself "Now I'm breathing in . . . now I'm breathing out . . ." Doing this will prevent you from analysing what you are doing or processing any other thoughts, which is an important feature of this activity. If a thought does come to mind, don't let it linger, just breathe it out and continue your deep breathing.

This is another reason why the practice of developing the awareness muscle is so beneficial. You are putting your attention on those parts of yourself (your physical experience of an emotion) of which we are usually totally unaware. I recommend to my clients, those who have a tendency to get overwhelmed by their emotions or who feel stress on a regular basis, that they build this practice into their daily routine.

This is, of course, what meditation is. However, I am cautious of using the 'M' word to clients, as many people still have a view that meditation is something a bit odd and mystical and is not appropriate in the business world. This is fine, and I never try to persuade them otherwise. Sometimes, I refer to it jokingly as "the deep breathing that we are *not* going to call meditation". Sometimes the client is very happy to be odd and mystical and call it meditation, in which case I might give them a few more guidelines on meditating, such as:

- You do not need to learn a technique. Our bodies are made to meditate and will take to it like a duck to water
- Do it with no expectation of feeling anything profound
- Just focus on 'being in your body' in the same way that you have been doing as you develop your awareness muscle
- Feel the sensation of what it feels like to breathe in and then breathe out
- Be the observer of yourself as you sit and breathe
- If you start thinking thoughts, do not beat yourself up, just return to observing your breathing as soon as you realise that you have slipped back into thought
- Keep your back straight and place your hands on your knees or thighs, rather than crossing them, to help the energy flow
- You can meditate for years and have no mystical experience and this, too, is great.

This is one of the most powerful things you can do for yourself in life. Deepak Chopra once said:

"All of our troubles and all of our anxieties stem from our inability to sit quietly in a room for ten minutes each day."

Tool Five: focusing

I said that there are two things you can do when the emotions are raging or even just muttering. Deep breathing is one of them and many people are well aware of it. The other thing is pretty much like magic and very few people are aware of it, even though it is as simple as breathing. Try it with me now. It is a bit tricky to do at the same time as reading the page so, if there happens to be someone else close by, perhaps you could ask them to talk you through it. Otherwise, read it first and then try it out.

Think about something that is going on in your life right now and makes you feel a little anxious. Not the great big, looming thing that might reduce you to tears, just a little anxiety-generating thing for the moment.

Consider the following:

- Whereabouts do you feel it in your body? Chest, solar plexus, stomach, throat or shoulders?
- What is the physical sensation of this in your body? Describe the physical feeling.
- How big is it?
- What colour is it?
- What texture is it? Hard, soft, spiky, smooth, fluffy or dense?
- Does it make a noise?
- Is it saying anything to you?

When you have located it and can describe its characteristics in these physical terms, without using emotionally descriptive words like panicky, angry, sad and so on, just focus your attention on it, in the same way that you focused on the feeling of 'hand' in Chapter Five. Put all your attention on it, without engaging your brain or thinking any thoughts about it. Do not start asking yourself "I wonder why it's orange and spiky. What does that mean?" Just feel the physical feeling of it in your body and see what happens.

After a minute or so (perhaps less), you may find that it changes its location, shape, size, texture or any of the characteristics. If so, then just focus on the new iteration of it in the same way as before, with the brain disengaged. It may change again once or twice more, but keep focusing on it wherever it moves to or whatever it feels like. After a little while, you will find that it disappears! It may possibly have disappeared straight away without changing shape.

How amazing is this? You can dissolve an emotion in a couple of minutes!

Astounding as it may appear, this is how we are made. This is a normal and natural part of our functioning and it will always work in this way within us.

The following conversation is a typical example of how this might play itself out as you coach someone through the use of this tool.

> Client: I feel anxious at the thought of asking my boss for a pay rise.
> You: Where do you feel this in your body?
> Client: In my stomach.
> You: What sort of shape is it?
> Client: Roundish.
> You: How big is it?
> Client: About the size of a football.
> You: What colour is it?
> Client: Grey.
> You: What kind of texture is it? What does it feel like to the touch?
> Client: It's spongy and light.

You: Is it making any noise at all?

Client: No.

You: Is it saying anything to you? This is not the same question as the last one.

Client: No, I don't think so.

You: Ok. So just put your attention on it and feel the feeling of it. Experience the sensation of it, what it feels like physically. Don't think any thoughts about it. Just disengage your brain. Don't try to analyse it in any way. Just feel it in your body. (This shouldn't sound like a list of instructions. You say this in a soft, relaxing way. Perhaps pausing a little between statements, so they are able to do it while you're still talking.

(Then, after a little while, twenty or thirty seconds or so . . .)

You: And tell me if anything happens to it.

(Leave plenty of space for them to go into this, while keeping your eyes on them. Even if they have their eyes closed, the client needs to feel your total engagement with them in this process and this will be interrupted if you take your eyes off them, whether they can see you or not. Then, after a little while more . . .)

Client: It's moved further down now.

You: What shape it is now?

Client: It's smaller, kind of flat.

You: Right. So, now just focus on that in the same way as you did before. Put all your attention on it and feel it. Tell me if it changes any more.

(After a little while more . . .)

Client: It's getting smaller and lighter. And it's yellow now.

You: Now, just focus on that.

Client: It's saying "It's ok now." And now it's not there any more.

This shows how effectively the body can handle troubling emotions, and is one of the most significant techniques that I use in coaching. It shows how safe we can be when we allow our bodies to go into this kind of 'process' and work on our issues with our brain disengaged. It is our brain that contaminates the process when we think about our issues, and this limits us enormously.

This is the same process that was at work in the 'well of pain', though at the time I had no idea that I had stumbled on such a profound truth about how our bodies work. The emotion is in the present moment and when you experience it, simply for what it is without interpreting it and making it mean anything or linking it to anything that happened in the past or might happen in the future, you are actually accepting it with no resistance and this is what causes it to melt away. Our natural default setting is health and happiness and, if you put your body in the right circumstances, it will automatically move you towards health and happiness. The present moment is always the right circumstance for dealing with unhelpful emotions uncontaminated with thoughts, logic, worries or historical 'evidence'.

Some points to bear in mind when leading someone through this process

1. I have given you a typical script so you can see how to work with a client using this technique. Later on, in further examples or in the case studies, I will not take you through each scenario in this step-by-step way. I may, for example, describe a session like the above focusing session by summarising it in this way:

> *The client described the feeling as being roundish and like a football in shape and size, making no noise. As he focused on it, it changed and became smaller, flatter and lighter and turned yellow before murmuring gently "It's ok now."*

However, even though I may write about it here in this way, during the session itself I will have asked the client all the questions, one at a time in the way I have illustrated. And I recommend that you do this. Do not just ask the client to "tell you all about the feeling" without these prompts. You are creating the space for the process. It is the process that is working within them, not the answers to the questions.

2. The questions about size and shape and colour may affect each other. For instance, if the client says it is the size of a football, you do not need to ask what shape it is. If they say it is the size of an apple, they may then perceive the colour as green or red and that is fine too. None of this matters, because the shape, size and colour do not necessarily mean anything. They are just ways of getting a handle on it as a physical entity.

3. To 'focus' does not mean to focus your thoughts on it but rather to direct your attention towards it. Thoughts are not involved in this process.

Once you have introduced clients to focusing in this way, it becomes a tool for them to use. I always ask them to develop the practice of using this technique whenever they feel an unhelpful emotion surfacing. Then I follow this up at future sessions by asking them to tell me about their experiences with it. I also give them this checklist of the steps to follow:

- Focus on how the emotion feels
- Put all your attention on it
- Be aware of:
    - where it is in your body
    - how big it is
    - what colour it is
    - what texture and shape it has
    - what noise it's making
    - what it might be saying

- Without trying to work out what it means, just continue to focus on it until you feel it changing its characteristics and its location

- As it does so, simply shift your attention and focus on the new version of it in exactly the same way

- It may change several times more, so just keep focusing on the new iterations of it, until finally it is no longer there.

As I mentioned in Chapter Two, this technique is essentially that described by Eugene Gendlin in his book *Focusing* and is also drawn from Brandon Bays' *The Journey*. Both of these books are included in the reading list at the end of this book, and I really do highly recommend that you read them both. I explained earlier that I use a version of this process that is less structured than those of Gendlin or Bays and, as you will see in Chapter Nine and onwards, it enables an exploration of the client's issue to go wherever it needs to rather than containing it within the focusing protocol.

Terry's magic headache cure

So, this technique illustrates how, in focusing your attention on troublesome emotions or emotional pain, you can dissolve them. Physical pain can often respond in the same way and you may have already experienced being able to reduce pain using a method like this. My husband, Terry, taught me this simple process for curing a headache. You can do it on yourself but here is a description of how to use it to help someone else. Ask the person with the headache the following questions:

> Where is the headache exactly? Don't point it out with your finger, just describe the position.
>
> What colour is it?
>
> How much water does it hold?
>
> So you really want it to go, do you?

Now where is it? (This step is a key one. If they find that it has moved, they are really working with the process. If not, then it might not work on them, they may not be totally engaged with it. Do not tell them this, though, as it will sound like a criticism. Just continue with the process and they may get into it later. If not, well, it just does not work for them, that's all.)

What colour is it now?

How much water does it hold?

And you *really* want it to go?

After two or three iterations of this, they usually find that it holds less and less water and eventually they cannot find it any more. Hey presto!

Before we leave this chapter on managing emotions, here is a little stand-alone exercise that incorporates the use of the awareness muscle, E+R=O, deep breathing and focusing. Try it for yourself for a couple of weeks and then offer it to your clients.

How often do you get irritated? You know, that little flicker of annoyance that ignites inside you when somebody barges past you in the street or jumps the queue in front of you. You cannot find your key. It starts to rain and you do not have your umbrella with you. The customer service representative is unhelpful *yet again*. You have forgotten to bring an important document with you to a meeting. Another driver cuts in front of you on the motorway. The feeling rises up within your chest and erupts into an exclamation such as "Oh no!" "Huh!" Hrrrmph!" or "Thank *you*, *very* much!" It feels inconsequential and passes quite quickly without disturbing your day very much. But it does disturb your energy and that of others around you through the quantum soup and the good news is that you can give it up. Easily.

Just notice it and then simply let it go. As soon as your awareness muscle tells you that you are having the sensations of irritation (probably somewhere around your gut and then rising upwards) because of the way you have just mentally labelled something or someone, spend the next few seconds noticing it, breathe out slowly and allow a little smile to happen inside you. (You may even find an actual smile erupting on your face too.) Then let it go, do not hook into it. Just give it up. Give up being irritated.

Allowing yourself to get irritated is a choice and you can stop making that choice. Each time you manage to achieve this silent, private success it will make you smile and no one else will know that you have just experienced an inner triumph over your emotions in this way. Now, to give up being irritated ever, is, I admit, quite a lofty goal and few will achieve this. Nevertheless, I continue to maintain it as a goal that I am drawing nearer to.

After a few weeks of practising this, on those occasions when you do hook into irritation, you will notice it quite strongly and will probably feel that you have let yourself down. This is a very simple exercise but one that has the power to transform. All those little moments of irritation cause far more damage than we might think. When you release yourself from them and fully accept the present moment with all its imperfections, something magical starts to happen. I will talk a little more about this idea of not resisting the way things are in Chapter Eighteen.

PART THREE

Working with the Tool Kit

CHAPTER NINE

Energy in our bodies

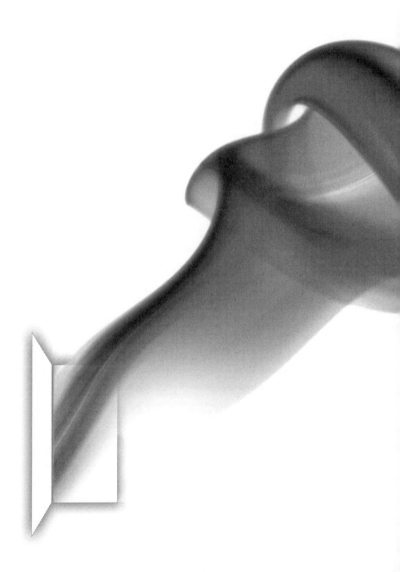

The body-mind

We have seen that every thing is made of energy – objects, thoughts, intent, emotions – everything. And so are events. The 'energy forms' or energetic footprint of all the events that we have ever experienced are lodged in the energy form that we call our body. They are housed there, energetically. Every joy, every disappointment, every expectation that was met or unmet, every argument, every relationship, every accident or success is still within the energy of our body.

We all know how, when we bring to mind an event that took place in the past, we might feel a corresponding sensation in our body. A tinge of embarrassment, a stab of pain, a surge of joy, a pin-prick of longing – it's still there able to have an effect on us after all these years and long after we think it was important to us. Sometimes we can be surprised to find that the memory of even a relatively insignificant event can trigger a response in us years later.

This is how we are made and is part of the human condition. It is also a portal for us to work with, a portal through which we can gain access to the mysterious workings of the body-mind. This means that, when we need to find the answer to a problem or issue, the most effective way is to go into our body and explore it from within rather than ask the brain, which is limited by memories of the past, predictions about the future or limiting assumptions. Counselling and many traditional forms of psychotherapy will approach issues by asking the mind-that-is-in-the-brain about the problem or the events that caused them. Because, as we saw in Chapter Five, this can generate a series of secondary emotions, which in their turn need to be explored, the process can take a long time and often does not result in the client feeling free from the grip of the emotion.

The concept of 'mind' is a curious one. Scientists cannot fully agree on what 'mind' is or where to look for it, though many think that the brain is a good starting place. It is certainly true

that there is a mind in the brain, but there is much evidence
also to suggest that this is not the only place where it lives.
As I have already mentioned, *The HeartMath Solution* by
Childre and Martin describes techniques for working with the
brain-in-the-heart, based on neurological research which
shows that the heart has an independent intelligence which
communicates with and influences the emotions and
perceptions.

Everything is a hologram

In the same way, the body itself has a mind or an innate
intelligence within every cell of itself that holds all the
information about the body. Many types of natural healing
therapies, including reiki, are based upon this concept. I have
taken a basic training in a form of applied kinesiology called
'integrated healing', which taps into the body's own
intelligence to heal itself at a physical, emotional and
spiritual level. In a seminar several years ago, I heard Deepak
Chopra, a foremost leader in mind-body medicine, say
"Everything is a hologram." I jotted this down, knowing at the
time that there was more to this statement than I then
understood. Since then, reading books such as Michael
Talbot's remarkable work, *The Holographic Universe*, I have
glimpsed more and more layers of the meaning of this
statement. A hologram is an image, every part of which
contains all of the information about the whole image. You
can break it into a thousand pieces and each piece will show
the whole picture. If an individual person is a hologram,
every part of that person will contain all the information about
him or her.

A palm reader, from studying your palm, can intuit your past
life events, your future life, your state of health, how many
children you have and so on. An iridologist gazing into your
iris can see similar information and a reflexologist can tell
your whole history from feeling the soles of your feet. In fact,

there are numerous types of therapeutic specialists who can examine one aspect of your body and see there the whole of your medical history. The medical intuitive, Caroline Myss, is able to do this, not only by simply looking at a person but also at a distance, without seeing them. Stanley Keleman, author of *Emotional Anatomy,* is a pioneer in the study of the body's physical connection to the emotional and psychological aspects of our human experience. His profound work shows how the very shape and structure of our body is formed from the emotions we have experienced from our earliest days.

Within each system, each organ, each scrap of tissue, each cell of the body is the information about the whole of the body. However, this holographic theory does not just apply to people: there is a sense in which a family, an organisation, the planet, a problem are all holograms. For example, when you telephone or walk through the doors of any organisation, how often do you find that the attitude of the person on the switchboard or at the reception desk represents how the whole organisation operates, serves the customer or does business? An attitude of indifference, welcome, sorry-no-can-do or superciliousness? All are reflected in every part of the company.

So everything about a person, the way they walk, the words they use, their facial expression, their health, their voice, contains a wealth of information about that person. Caroline Myss says in her book, *Anatomy of the Spirit,* that "Our biography becomes our biology." Our body is made up of the energy of the events we have experienced, and the issues and problems caused by those events are accessible to us through the portal of the body itself. When we ask the body about the issues that are troubling or inhibiting us in some way, the answers emerge with purity and clarity, unencumbered by the false assumptions of the brain and usually in the form of metaphor. People often feel that, because they have had a problem for twenty or thirty years, it would require a proportional number of years to explore and resolve it. This is not so. This process can take you directly to the heart of the matter like a knife through butter – simply, straightforwardly and, for the most part, painlessly.

Using the focusing technique to explore an issue

We have seen how we can dissolve away troublesome emotions by focusing on them and experiencing the physical sensation of the emotion within our body. This is one way of using the focusing technique. Another valuable tool for working with emotions, based on this technique, is called 'metaphorical journeying'.

Metaphor is a very natural and easy way for us to look at what is happening to us. It taps into our natural child nature and allows a story to unfold without our consciously thinking about how to tell it. When we allow ourselves to think in metaphor, some interesting insights pop into being, insights that connect with an inner, well-defended part of ourselves that we cannot normally access. It is an approach used in some fields of psychotherapy and it is commonplace in family therapy. I came across specific techniques for working with metaphor through psychodrama training, from where it found its way into my coaching practice.

This is an example of how to explore an issue using metaphorical journeying. Here I was working with Michael, who had attended a coaching skills training course for leaders with me and who I worked with afterwards on some leadership coaching for himself. He is a very practical, cognitive, technically-minded guy, not given to whimsicality or airy-fairy nonsense!

Case Study One

Michael tells me that he is not able to use his coaching techniques on himself for self-coaching.

Annette: What is stopping you from self-coaching?

Michael: It is a kind of blockage.

Annette: Whereabouts do you feel it in your body?

Michael: Around my abdomen.

(I asked the focusing questions about size, colour, shape and so on that I described in the last chapter. As I mentioned then, I asked all these questions one at a time, and in the next line of this dialogue I am summarising his replies.)

Michael: It's the size of a melon. It's cancerous, red, amorphous, blobby, squidgy.

Annette: Does it make a noise?

Michael: No, but it haunts me and taunts me.

Annette: How?

Michael: It tells me that I'll be found out. It says that I have to do what it tells me so that I won't look like a twit.

Annette: How long has it been there?

Michael: As long as I can remember.

Annette: What is its weak spot?

Michael: It's that I don't want it there.

Annette: If you don't want it there, why is it still there?

Michael: I let it stay.

Annette: What is the pay-off for letting it stay? What does it allow you to do or allow you not to do?

Michael: It stops me from failing. It drives me. It yells at me – loudly at certain times like an alarm clock so that I won't look like a twit. This is the worst thing that can happen in this organisation. It stops me from being shoddy.

Annette: It seems to be doing some good work for you. Could you do these things for yourself without it?

Michael: No, it's a form of conscience. It's happy; it knows I'm frightened of it. It wants to be taken notice of and these are its tactics to get noticed.

Annette: How might it look if you weren't frightened of it?

Michael: It would be a brass bell ringing to warn me. It would motivate me. It would drive me. It would help me not to look like a prat.

Annette: What would make it feel good?

Michael: If it were listened to. If it were taken notice of. If we were friends.

Annette: What do you think it wants to say to you?

Michael: I don't know.

Annette: How would it be if you were friends?

Michael: We'd be in the same team.

Annette: Does it trust you?

Michael: (He immediately answered.) No, of course not! It thinks I've got further than I deserve. It knows me. It's not jealous though. It thinks I wouldn't be competent without it. It's not a separate personality from me. It never comes out of its place.

Annette: If it's done all that, and is still doing it for you, and you can't work without it (therefore, you need it) and you think it wants to be listened to, then possibly it wants to be recognised for its good work and for you to thank it. It's possibly a bit grumpy that its efforts are not being recognised and rewarded.

Michael: Yes, I think this might be true.

(At this point we also had a short conversation about the weirdness of this line of exploration. As we discussed it ('the blob'), I asked Michael if he wanted to give it a name other than 'the blob'. He suggested Rupert.)

Annette: Can I ask you to try something now?

Michael: OK, sure.

Annette: I'd like you to focus on the gifts and talents you've been given. You have great intelligence and intellectual abilities, enormous creativity and you've been blessed with good health. Just become aware of them and feel in your body and in your heart a real sense of gratitude for them.

(He did this for a few minutes.)

Annette: Now I'd like you to send this sense of gratitude
down through you to envelope Rupert. Express your
gratitude to him for what he has done for you as well.

Even though Michael found this quite hard to do, perhaps not
surprisingly, I encouraged him to work on doing this regularly
before our next session. In future sessions, we worked on
developing Michael's relationship with Rupert even further and
Michael began to learn how they could help and support each
other.

* * *

So, what on earth is happening here? If you have never met
this sort of approach before, it could look pretty strange I will
admit. But once you get the sense of how the client's body-
mind is working, it will soon seem quite normal. I do not have
a neat explanation of exactly what is happening; nothing in
the quantum world does have such an explanation. But what I
understand of it is that Michael's inner wisdom, his 'higher
mind', which understood the inner tussle he was having with
himself over his fear that he was not as good as he thought
he was, was not accessible to his conscious mind. If we had
tried to access Michael's inner wisdom by asking his conscious
mind questions, we would probably have hit the smokescreen
that he was already facing and got no further. This is how our
minds work when we try to work out a problem that is
niggling away at us.

Before we look at this case study in more depth, I will spend
a few moments describing the way that our thinking limits our
ability to solve our own problems, as Michael had been
experiencing.

Piles of sand

The human brain is like a pile of sand. If you take a pile of
sand and pour a glass of water over it, the water will form
pathways down the side of the pile. If you take a second

glass of water and pour it over the pile of sand, most of the water will run down the preformed pathways. It may form one or two more but that is all. If you take a third glass of water and pour it over the sand, all the water will run down the already formed pathways. The sand is incapable of forming any new pathways.

This is what happens in our brain when we think about a problem or an issue confronting us. The first time we think about it, the thoughts we generate form neural pathways in the brain. These are actual, physical grooves in the brain that represent the thought. (Maybe this is what we mean by 'a train of thought'.) The second time we think about the problem, most of our thinking will go down and reinforce the same pathways, though we may get one or two new ideas. By the time we churn it over the third or the thirty-third or the three-hundred-and-thirty-third time (as we tend to do), we have rendered the pathways into deeply established furrows and our brain is incapable of thinking about the problem in a new way. We may get variations on the old themes but nothing really new. As Einstein said "We need a different mind-set to solve a problem from the one we had when we created it."

So we need to be able to create a new pile of sand to think about a problem in a fresh way. Quantum skills can help to do this, particularly when using the metaphorical journeying tool. We protect ourselves from our 'inner knowing' about the nature of our problems or limitations because we fear that we will not be able to handle it if we know the truth. What we do not realise is that "the truth will set us free" as the good book says. Metaphor makes it safe for us to work with the unsayable – "I am not as good as I think I am", "People see me as incompetent", "They're all really laughing at me."

Analysis of the case study

As you can imagine, when someone is being coached using the approach in the above case study for the first time, they are often a bit surprised to find themselves having a conversation with what feels like an 'entity' within their body. Yet, strangely enough, people move into it quite easily and with no resistance. Sometimes, as Michael did here, they will say "This is a bit weird. Is this normal?" a few minutes into the journey. And once you have reassured them that it is perfectly normal they step back into it again. And, of course, it is normal. Just a different kind of 'normal'.

To learn enough from the explanations and the case studies in this book to be able to work with this tool yourself, it will probably be useful to analyse this journey so that you can see at what points, as the coach, you might intervene to move the journey forward. I have added relevant comments in bold tinted text in brackets. Some of these may be very obvious to you as a coach, but please bear with me if I include them for the benefit of readers who may not be experienced coaches. The most significant points, though, are those where I make an intuitive leap in my questioning. Perhaps we might call this a quantum leap? This is where I ask a question that is not directly suggested by something that the client said but something that just occurs to me as being a fruitful avenue for exploration. I will not try to offer an explanation as to where it comes from but leave it to you to 'feel' what sparked the intuition. We will examine later in more detail the significant role that intuition plays in practising quantum skills for coaches, and how you can learn to trust your intuition to guide you through metaphorical journeying.

> Annette: What is stopping you from self-coaching?
> Michael: It is a kind of blockage.
> Annette: Whereabouts do you feel it in your body?
> Michael: Around my abdomen.

(I asked more focusing questions about size, colour, shape and so on that I described in the last chapter. As I mentioned then, I asked all these questions one at a time, and in the next line of this dialogue I am summarising his replies.)

Michael: It's the size of a melon. It's cancerous, red, amorphous, blobby, squidgy.

(Even though this description sounds quite dramatic, particularly the word 'cancerous', I did not feel that I needed to explore this. The description is simply the client's way of visualising the emotion. 'Cancerous' sounds like a judgement about the emotion and we are not working with the client's judgement, just their observations and experiences. If you respond by being shocked or upset by this, it might worry the client and inhibit him from articulating further metaphorical insights.)

Annette: Does it make a noise?

Michael: No, but it haunts me and taunts me.

(Explore what he means by this.)

Annette: How?

Michael: It tells me that I'll be found out. It says that I have to do what it tells me so that I won't look like a twit.

Annette: How long has it been there?

(This is just one of the possible ways of exploring this answer. There is no one 'right answer' in any of this. I might also have asked, always using the same words that the client had used, "What is it telling you to do", "Why does it want to protect you from looking like a twit", "What does it think you'll be found out about?")

Michael: As long as I can remember.

Annette: What is its weak spot?

(This is the intuitive leap, the quantum leap, not based on anything that the client has already said, which leads to a series of fruitful insights.)

Michael: It's that I don't want it there.

Annette: If you don't want it there, why is it still there?

(More useful than asking "why don't you want it there?" because it moves the story on rather than going back over

ground that he has already covered by implication when he
talked about how it yells at him.)

Michael: I let it stay.

Annette: What is the pay-off for letting it stay? What does it
allow you to do or what does it allow you not to do?
(It is always useful to bear in mind that we do certain things
because they serve us in some way and there is some benefit
or pay-off to be gained. Sometimes these things serve us in
ways that inhibit our growth, and this may simply be because
we do not feel ready to grow in that way. There is no blame or
criticism attached to this. But, when you hear clients talking
about why they do things that do not seem to serve them, it is
always useful to explore what's in it for them, to flag up for
them that they are internally consenting to this.)

Michael: It stops me from failing. It drives me. It yells at me
– loudly at certain times like an alarm clock so that I
won't look like a twit. This is the worst thing that can
happen in this organisation. It stops me from being
shoddy.

Annette: It seems to be doing some good work for you.
Could you do these things for yourself without it?
(Another quantum leap here.)

Michael: No, it's a form of conscience. It's happy; it knows
I'm frightened of it. It wants to be taken notice of and
these are its tactics to get noticed.

Annette: How might it look if you weren't frightened of it?

Michael: It would be a brass bell ringing to warn me. It
would motivate me. It would drive me. It would help me
not to look like a prat.

Annette: What would make it feel good?
(Another quantum leap here. This is sparked by a sense of the
client needing to integrate this 'blob' into himself and the next
few questions also reflect this. I will talk more about
integration later in this chapter.)

Michael: If it were listened to. If it were taken notice of. If
we were friends.

Annette: What do you think it wants to say to you?

Michael: I don't know.

Annette: How would it be if you were friends?

Michael: We'd be in the same team.

Annette: Does it trust you?

> **(Another quantum leap based on the idea Michael is developing that there might be a possibility of a friendship in this antagonistic relationship. For there to be a friendship, there would first need to be a level of trust.)**

Michael: (He immediately answered.) No, of course not! It thinks I've got further than I deserve. It knows me. It's not jealous though. It thinks I wouldn't be competent without it. It's not a separate personality from me. It never comes out of its place.

> **(Here he is giving quite a lot of information about what he thinks 'the blob' feels – this is very useful information.)**

Annette: If it's done all that, and is still doing it for you, and you can't work without it, which means you need it, and you think it wants to be listened to, then possibly it wants to be recognised for its good work and for you to thank it. It's possibly a bit grumpy that its efforts are not being recognised and rewarded.

Michael: Yes, I think this might be true.

> (At this point we also had a short conversation about the weirdness of this line of exploration. As we discussed it ('the blob'), I asked him if he wanted to give it a name other than 'the blob'. He suggested 'Rupert'.)

Annette: Can I ask you to try something now?

Michael: OK, sure.

Annette: I'd like you to focus on the gifts and talents you've been given. You have great intelligence and intellectual abilities, enormous creativity and you've been blessed with good health. Just become aware of them and feel in your body and in your heart a real sense of gratitude for them.

> **(This is a major quantum leap and totally driven by Michael's need to integrate Rupert within himself as happened in the next exercise that I asked him to do.)**

> (He did this for a few minutes.)

> Annette: Now I'd like you to send this sense of gratitude
> down through you to envelope Rupert. Express your
> gratitude to him for what he has done for you as well.

I mentioned in an earlier chapter that when someone first
suggested that I write a book or run workshops on quantum
skills for coaches, one of the reasons I was dubious was that I
did not know if I could articulate what it was that I did
precisely enough to be able to convey it to others. I did not
know what it was that I knew. And I am finding this out all the
time.

It was as if this way of working 'found me'. It 'landed on me'
and I found myself working with it intuitively before really
understanding where it came from. One of the things I learnt
during an early quantum skills workshop, as students asked
questions about the case studies, was about the role of
integration.

Integration

When a person suffers some form of trauma, shock or any
minor event that threatens their sense of self, their energetic
body often responds by cutting off or fragmenting a part of
themselves and keeping this part separate from their
conscious sense of self. This can be the result of their
feelings, such as:

- Shame at having allowed this trauma to occur, for
  example as in any form of abuse
- Anger
- Rejection
- Embarrassment or humiliation
- Sorrow.

It is an internal mechanism to protect the client's sense of self
from feeling they have failed or are 'less than' they would
want. As you explore an issue through metaphorical

journeying, it often happens that the fragmented part of the self starts to speak, perhaps because it feels safe in the world of metaphor, as if it is wearing a mask and can speak without being identified. It often happens that this part enters into a dialogue with the person or even with another part of the self, so you may find yourself facilitating a conversation between two or more different aspects of the client.

I had been working in this way for years before realising that the 'intuitive leaps' I make in facilitating these metaphorical journeys often come from an unconscious pull within me to help to integrate this fragmented part of the self into the 'whole being' of the client.

This rather wonderfully illustrates that you do not need to understand with your head why something is working or to give it a label. If you are working with the body, in the flow of the journey, no explanation is necessary. And, of course, you do not need to explain any of this to clients: it will reek of psychobabble! They will just be marvelling at the ability of their body to surface and deal with their deepest issues. This is enough for them and had been for me until the 'integration' idea emerged, offering me new insights into this marvellous process.

Applied kinesiology

Applied kinesiology (AK) is the study of muscles and the relationship of muscle strength to health, which involves manual muscle testing. Applied kinesiology is based on the theory that an organ dysfunction is accompanied by a specific muscle weakness. Diseases and disorders are diagnosed through muscle-testing procedures and then treated. It is not the same as kinesiology, or biomechanics, which is the scientific study of movement. There are some significant applications of this to the way in which we look at our lives and face our problems, and some coaches use applications of AK to work with their clients.

It is a fascinating area of research, medical treatment, therapy and ultimately spiritual teaching, which I only really touch upon in quantum skills even though I have acquired a basic qualification in one of the many forms of applied kinesiology. There is much more that I could embrace from this amazing field, and perhaps in the future I may do so. Everything in its time. However, I would thoroughly recommend that you read *Power vs Force*, a magnificent book by David Hawkins. It is not essential reading for learning the quantum skills but is absolutely fascinating and exhilarating.

I frequently show clients this exercise based on the central technique in AK – muscle-testing. (You do not have to use exactly the same words as I give here, but make sure that the words you do use convey the same meaning, with no hints or clues as to what will happen.)

1. Ask the client to stand straight, feet slightly apart for good balance. (You stand facing the client.)

2. Coach: Are you right-handed or left-handed?

   Client: Right-handed. (I will describe this exercise as if the client is right-handed. Just reverse the instructions for left-handed clients.)

   Coach: So, your right arm is probably your strongest arm?

   (The client will probably agree.)

3. Coach: I'd like you to think of something that makes you feel really, really happy. So happy that you can feel your feet growing right through the floor with sheer happiness. And when you're in this mode, I'm going to ask you to put your left arm out to the side like this.

   (Demonstrate with your left arm held out to the side, parallel to the floor, elbow straight.)

   Coach: I'm going to try to push your arm downwards and I want you to resist as hard as you can.

   (Check that the client has understood and is thinking about something that makes them feel really happy.

When the client puts their arm out to the side, place your right hand on the client's arm just above the wrist.)

4. Now, push down on the client's arm fairly quickly, firmly and evenly. You will probably find that their arm resists your push and feels strong. If it doesn't and falls to the side, check that the client really was thinking of something that made them feel happy. Sometimes people can't get into this mode very easily.

5. Coach: So, you can 'do' happy. Now I'd like to see if you can 'do' angry. Not a great big sense of anger against some kind of social injustice, but a simmering-on-the-back-burner kind of anger, perhaps a teeth-grinding sort of anger against some irksome individual who gets on your nerves. Then when you're in this mode I'd like you to put your right arm out this time. I'm going to push it down again and you're going to resist like you did last time. (Check the client has understood.)

6. Repeat the instruction in step 4. You will find that the client's arm has no resistance to your push and falls to the side easily. The client will be surprised, of course. Most people expect that they would be stronger when they are feeling angry, especially if they felt their jaw clenched at the time.

Then you debrief this together, bringing out the following main points.

1. This was the result you expected to see. It always happens like this. The only times it does not work is when the person is not really 'in the mode'.

2. When you are feeling happy, (and we are not talking a flimsy, happy-clappy kind of emotion, but a deep-rooted happiness), you are physically strong. Your body is likely to do a good job of resisting germs and bugs and will be strong and resilient. You are also more likely to be

mentally resilient and resourceful in dealing with problems and things going awry in your life.

3. But, when you are angry, you are not strong like this. (We are not talking about an anger towards some kind of great injustice. If your anger were directed against something that threatened the life of a loved one, you might have great strength, perhaps enough to raise a car off the ground.) When you feel this kind of irritation, or annoyance against someone, you become physically weaker than you might be and may catch colds or flu more often. But you are also likely to be less creative and resourceful around problem solving and dealing with difficult situations.

4. Whatever the thought was that made you feel so happy, it will always work for you in the same way. You can make yourself strong and resilient by choosing to think this thought. But you do have to make this choice, consciously. There is no 'thought fairy' fluttering around who will to do it for you or sprinkle 'thought dust' over you. You have to decide "At this moment I need to feel strong and resilient. So I'll think my happy thought, right now." And then do it.

This is a great tool to share with your clients, and I usually choose to do this if they are talking about their problem situation in a way that shows how helpless they feel. It is one of the ways of demonstrating to them the vital role that their thoughts play in the unfolding of their life situation. E+R=O is another tool that illustrates this.

CHAPTER TEN

The energy in words

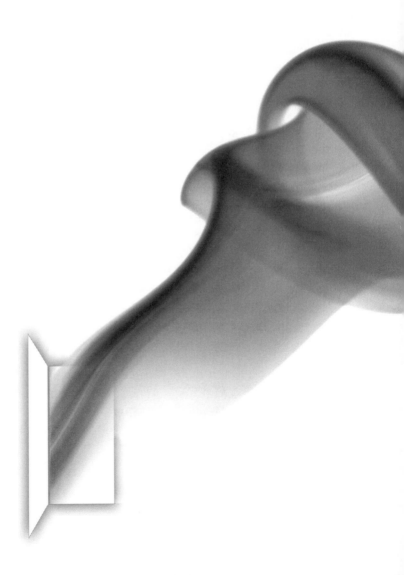

I said earlier, when talking about the holographic nature of the world, that everything about a person – the way they walk, the words they use, their facial expressions, their health, their voice – contains all the information about them. So, how can our words be a hologram?

When we utter a word, the energetic vibration of that word resonates in our body in the same way that a thought, a belief or an event resonates. And that resonance affects the rest of the body, because everything is connected. The word also affects others who may be near enough to hear it (in fact, it can affect them even if they cannot hear it, through the quantum soup). There is a sizeable body of evidence to suggest that the words of doctors, surgeons and nurses spoken to a patient (even when comatose or under anaesthesia) affect the patient's physical body and their ability to heal. Doctor and author Larry Dossey presents much of this evidence in his book *Healing Words*, as does the surgeon Bernie Siegel in his books *Love, Medicine and Healing* and *Peace, Love and Healing*.

We usually pay great attention to the food we ingest into our systems. We make sure that we eat food that is nourishing and wholesome, and generally try to avoid consuming poison! When we use words, we are, in effect, ingesting them into our systems in the same way as food and they have the ability to either nourish or poison us. Just as we become the thoughts that we think, our words also shape who we become. We all know people who are continually getting angry, or who regularly find themselves saying such things as "I find that extremely offensive", "How dare you say that to me!", "This is totally unacceptable", or who are always complaining about how bad things are or moaning about how difficult life is. If you think about all the people that you know who fall into these categories, you will probably also be aware of how their body, face, tone of voice and general energy reflect this way of looking at the world.

So, in the same way that we need to be responsible for the way in which we allow ourselves to think, we need to be rigorous in the way we use and ingest words. We always, always have a choice about the words we use to describe what is happening to us. This choice will produce a physiological change in our bodies, which will affect our ability to deal with the circumstance to an enormous degree.

The written word has as much power as the spoken word. When we read a book that we find uplifting, scary, stimulating, depressing, thrilling, challenging and so on, we are describing the effect the words have on us. This is why it is so beneficial to us to read uplifting books. Our bodies are receiving energetic nourishment from the words.

This is also what makes affirmations work and what makes them so powerful. Affirmations are positive statements that we make about ourselves or the way we see or experience life, and they have long been used by a variety of therapists with their clients.

Below are instructions for making affirmations that you may wish to pass on to your clients.

Affirmations

Write a paragraph describing yourself in the following way:

- Describe the most marvellous version of yourself that you can imagine, as if you or your life were already like this.

- Use the present tense, e.g. "I radiate love and kindness to everyone around me", "I am warm and caring", "I feel confidence and peace in every cell of my being."

- Describe your personal qualities – your attributes, abilities, the way you treat other people, the way you treat yourself, the effect you have on others and so on (even if you do not quite believe it to be true right now).

- Do not use any reducing qualifiers such as 'fairly', 'quite', 'not bad at . . .'

- Avoid using any negative language such as describing what you want to avoid doing or what you do not do. Describe what you *do* and what you *are*.

- Be totally unfettered and superlative.

- It should be so marvellous and shining that it will make your toes curl when you read it.

- When you have crafted it, write it on a piece of card.

- Read it first thing every morning, three times, out loud if possible, but in your head if you do not have that kind of privacy. The reason for this is that you will take these thoughts into the day with you.

- Do the same last thing at night, three times. This is important because it means that you will drop this message into your subconscious as you sleep and it will do its work while you are unaware of it.

- Your reading of this should be with meaning and feeling as if you believe it to be true.

- At odd moments during the day, take out your card and read it in your head, but still with feeling.

- Do this, without fail every day, even if you hit a low spot and find it hard to do.

- As you do this, smile to yourself.

Be aware of the effect this exercise has on you, how you feel and how different your way of thinking becomes. Observe and be aware also of how others react to you and notice if this is different from usual. Take an interest in this, treat it as research and observe the results with interest.

You can make affirmations about the way you see or experience life in the same way. Examples might be "I see only beauty in all the people in my life", "Life is a marvellous adventure", "I say 'yes' to everything that happens to me."

My own daily favourite and one that I say out loud in the shower most mornings is "Just for today, I live magically." After saying this to myself I expect to see magic happening all around me and am only disappointed when I forget to look for it!

In the last chapter we saw how our biography becomes our biology; so, then, do our words become our biology. In a sense, we *are* the words we say and think. This gives a new slant to Descarte's famous strapline, which might read "I think, and therefore I am what I think!" Of course, this too is only true in a certain sense, not ultimately. If we begin to look at who we are in a deeper, spiritual sense, it is not true that we are our thoughts. As spiritual teacher Eckhart Tolle teaches in *The Power of Now* and *A New Earth*, we are far greater than our thoughts, and our thoughts can, in fact, be the main impediment to finding our true self. However, leading the client down the spiritual path is not the brief of the coach unless they ask you for spiritual coaching and you feel called to, and able to, respond. In an everyday sense, it can be very helpful to the client to be aware of how our thoughts shape us physically and emotionally.

Contra-indications and negative scripting

Some clients, however, will find it extremely hard to make affirmations. For people who have developed strong patterns of negative self-talk, to make positive, shining statements about themselves is something that they have perhaps never done, and trying to do so can cause considerable distress. This may in part be due to the 'scripting' that they received early in their life from parents and other seniors, at school from their teachers and peers and in a variety of other life situations. Scripting starts in childhood with the strong family messages from our parents that shape our thinking and our values around various aspects of life. These messages form a kind of script for us that we repeat throughout our life. If this script works for us and serves us in our life, it can be seen as good, but if it works against us and disables us we may need to design a different script.

So the clients' scripts are sets of beliefs about themselves that they have heard from others and have become their own view, their own 'truth' about themselves. "You'll never amount to anything", "You're not as confident as your sister", even statements that may have a positive element to them such as "You're the brainy one in the family so don't worry that you're plain looking".

Of course, these scripts are not the truth, but holding onto them for years can create a self-fulfilling prophecy and give the impression that they are the truth, by producing the very 'evidence' that supports them. And this evidence just serves to 'prove' that it is the truth. As a coach, you will easily spot how your clients' scripting shapes their sense of self, or lack of it, and you can then work with them to develop their awareness of how their beliefs (made manifest through their thoughts and words) actually shape who they are. Once this awareness has started to germinate, you can continue to work to change the scripting into 'truths' that will serve the client and help them to step into their full power and find their 'castle'.

A suggested pathway to follow when you recognise negative scripting might be to help your client to:

- Recognise that this is a script
- Recognise that it is not working
- Choose a new script and cut loose from the old script
- Formulate a process to use the new script until becoming comfortable with it
- Expect it to feel uncomfortable at first and then gain confidence in stepping outside of their comfort zone.

A book that I regularly recommend to clients as we work on this area of their life is *The Hidden Messages in Water* by

Masuru Emoto. This extraordinary book, which I feel is more or less compulsory for anyone working in this area, describes the work of Emoto, a renowned Japanese physicist, and shows how human consciousness affects the vibration of water. Its implications for us are immensely important and exciting and will give you and your clients some interesting food for thought, particularly in connection with making affirmations. I will not describe it further here, but save the delight of the discovery to you as you read it and enjoy the astonishing photographs.

CHAPTER ELEVEN

Awareness of the energy of words in offering feedback

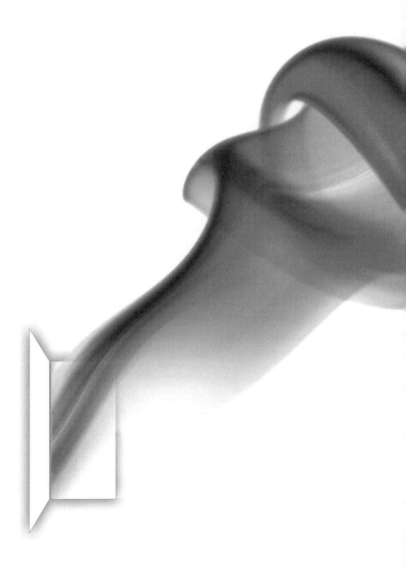

Having explored some elements of the energy of words, I will now look at the link between this and the notion that 'everything is a hologram', which we looked at in Chapter Nine. To recap a little, the holographic nature of everything means that every part of a particular thing, contains all of the information about the whole of it. Everything about a person – the way they walk, the words they use, their facial expressions, their health, their voice – contains all the information about that person. As a coach, of course, you observe and are aware of the information that clients give you through all of these aspects of themselves, which are valuable levers for an exploration of the way they feel about their issues and general approach to life.

As you observe these things, without drawing any conclusions or trying to interpret or make sense of it in any way, it can be very valuable to the client for you to offer your observation and feedback and then explore the response using quantum skills techniques. This process can help to identify and shift unhelpful, embedded patterns in the client's life.

Why offer feedback?

Feedback is valuable because the last thing we find out about ourselves is our impact on others. One of the central reasons that people seek coaching is that they are not getting the results in their life, or in some area of their life, that they really want. A common reason for this is that the impact of their behaviour or self-presentation on other people is working against them in some way.

We are all well aware of the impact of others upon us. For example, when a new person enters the room, we know just what it is that they bring with them that was not there before. We know the experience we are having when we are with them. And when they leave the room, we know what it is that they take away with them. But we do not know what our impact on others might be and what we bring into the room with us. In other words, we do not know what experience others are having of us. We might guess at it from the way they behave around us; this is the key indicator of our impact. But perhaps we are not skilled at observing others' responses to us. Perhaps it would be too painful to recognise what our impact might be or maybe we just have a self-protective need not to truly observe and learn from what we see.

This is true for many of us and so, although we *do* know that we are not getting the results we really want, we do *not* know what might turn things around for us if we were to do it differently. We do not know what we have to do to make sure that the experience other people have of us is positive and useful for them. People do not tell us. In fact, they usually do not even know what they would tell us because they do not know what it is that makes them feel uncomfortable, or anxious or impatient around us – they just sense it in their bodies and react to it.

It may even be that people present us with inauthentic behaviour in their reaction to us. For example, if we are their dominating, performance-driven boss, fear or anxiety may be their genuine reaction. However, to keep themselves safe and in our good graces, they may choose to conceal this behind a welcoming smile and light-hearted banter. This leads us to feel that our behaviour is having a positive effect on others and we might label it as 'firm but fair' and think of ourselves in this way.

People will always forget what you did. People will always forget what you said. But people will never forget how you made them feel.

How to offer feedback

Sometimes, if people feel sufficiently uncomfortable, anxious or impatient, they may give angry or frustrated feedback as an expression of these negative feelings. This is only likely to lead to confrontation, defensiveness or denial from the individual and is a far cry from the kind of constructive feedback that will result in the person deciding to examine and address the issue.

On the whole, most people are not skilled at giving feedback to others. They do not know the rules of feedback so are afraid of getting it wrong or upsetting the other person. It is risky to give feedback and so much easier to withdraw from the person by trying to minimise contact time with them. It may also feel presumptuous to offer this kind of information to another, particularly if not invited to do so. The person is unlikely to put themselves in the awkward position of asking "So, what do you think about me?" or "How do I come over to you?" This would seem too weird. And the result of all this is that the person is not getting the results they want in their life. So, to give someone feedback is to offer a gift. The crucial thing is to give it in such a way that it *feels* like a gift and will be of benefit to them, and there are a few basic rules to help in this. Now I am absolutely sure that, as a coach, you are quite familiar with the feedback process so this will be a repetition of what you know already. Please bear with me as I outline the rules here, for the benefit of any reader who is not a coach or who may be uncertain about this delicate subject.

The rules of giving feedback

1. The feedback should *always* be for the benefit of the other person.
2. Give feedback about *behaviour* that you have observed.
3. Ask permission to give the feedback.
4. Describe your observations without evaluating, labelling or judging them in any way.
5. Give the feedback as soon as possible after the behaviour has happened.

6. Only give feedback about something that the person can change.
7. Remember that a fault is simply an overuse of a quality.
8. Remember also that the feedback says more about you than it does about the other person.

Let's look at these in a little more detail.

1. *The feedback should always be for the benefit of the other person*

In Chapter Two we looked at the power of our intent in any situation. Because of the nature of the quantum soup, everything is connected and the other person or people will sense our true intent, however skilful our attempts at disguising it from them or from ourselves. So, before offering the gift of feedback, go inside yourself, examine your intent scrupulously to ensure that there is not the tiniest trace of a desire to score a point. Make sure your intent is pure.

2. *Give feedback about behaviour that you have observed*

This is the whole point of feedback. You are making observations about what you have seen and experienced and perhaps the impact that this has upon you. You cannot offer useful feedback about something that you have heard others say or a conclusion you have reached about someone's behaviour. This becomes mere hearsay or your opinion. The person will be likely to refute it, and rightly so.

To link this with the above rule, do not forget that the feedback is only describing the behaviour, not the person. For example, people who behave in ways that focus attention on themselves are doing simply that. It does not mean that these people are self-centred; it is not *who they are*. If you do not fully believe this, they will hear this judgement from you when you describe their 'attention-seeking' behaviour. In the coaching process, you will doubtless explore what is driving this behaviour and may find some cause dating back to childhood, such as having been a middle child in a large family where there was a dearth of parental attention.

3. *Ask permission to offer the feedback*

In a first meeting with a client, most coaches describe the coaching process and their own methods and, jointly with the client, design and agree the way they will work together. This is a good time to let the client know that you may, from time to time, ask if they would like some feedback from you to help them achieve their coaching goals. In my experience, the client is always happy to agree to this. As we have discussed, people rarely get the feedback they need and want from others, and they see this as an opportunity to learn about themselves. Having prepared them for this aspect of the coaching process, you then have permission to ask if you could make an observation whenever you feel that it would be useful and appropriate.

4. *Describe your observations without evaluating, labelling or judging them in any way*

This is an extension of the second rule. It is unwise to interpret or label what you see and assume that it means something. *Everything is information, and it doesn't necessarily mean what you think or necessarily mean anything at all.* Examples of giving a behaviour a label might be to think that someone is arrogant, has no 'sense of self', is not a contributor or is a bully. So, take care to describe the behaviour without drawing any conclusions or trying to interpret or make sense of it in any way as this will seriously limit the way you might then work with a client.

We only work with what is, what we see in the present. Everything else is interpretation and potentially flawed. You may ask "What is the difference between labelling and listening to what your intuition is telling you" as the difference can sometimes look quite subtle. I will be talking more about intuition in Chapter Fifteen as well as giving examples of how I have used it in specific case studies, so I hope that the difference will become clear.

5. *Give the feedback as soon as possible after the behaviour has happened*

If it is a behavioural pattern rather than a one-off action, wait for an occasion when the client demonstrates the behaviour and then, if the moment is appropriate, give your feedback about it. The client's body will still be resonating with the sensation of having just done it. You can then work with the client, through the medium of their awareness muscle, to explore the behaviour. Everything is energy. Since the client's body-mind remembers the energy of the behaviour, and they will recognise the effect of it within their own body, there is a greater chance that the exploration will be immediate, relevant and interesting to them. For an illustration of this, see the story of Tony later in Chapter Thirteen.

6. *Only give feedback about something that the person can change*

This is obvious but worth mentioning anyway. Feedback is about behaviour. Since a lot of behaviour is unconscious, habitual and instinctive, people often believe that they cannot change such ingrained behaviour. This is why coaching was invented! As we have seen so far in this book, when we become aware of those things that we are not usually aware of, such as our thought patterns and emotions, we are less controlled by them and can bring about changes in them. Giving feedback about the behavioural manifestations of thought patterns and emotions and their impact can be useful. There are, though, some things about a person's impact on others that they cannot change, such as physical attributes or regional accent. So while you might usefully give someone feedback about the speed of their speech or the kind of words they habitually use, telling them that you find it hard to understand their accent is not useful!

7. Remember that a fault is simply an overuse of a quality

Our faults or things we do not like about ourselves are actually qualities that we are overusing or using inappropriately in a particular situation. It is as if the volume has been turned up too high and there is just too much of it blasting out of us. If we can just learn to turn down the volume a little, we can see that these so-called weaknesses are in fact our greatest assets and can become tools that can work for us instead of against us.

For example, a naturally enthusiastic person, whose flow of enthusiasm is overly accentuated, may come across as being 'in your face' to others. Someone who is well-organised may seem controlling if this quality is inappropriately used. An overuse of the quality of positive-thinking can appear insensitive to others who may see themselves trapped in a dismal reality. An overemphasis of focus on achieving results in your life can feel like perfectionism to those around you and a passion for something may look uncomfortably like zeal.

Tell this to your clients; it will serve to reassure them and enable them to see themselves in a different light, and to understand why they are perhaps sometimes praised for these characteristics and sometimes vilified for them. Always bear this in mind as you give clients feedback about their impact. It will help you to see the greatness in them.

8. *Remember that the feedback says more about you than it does about the other person*

This relates back to the first rule, examine your intent. The way you choose to present your observations – the words you use, the tone of your voice, the compassion or lack of it that you feel for the other person – will all have an impact on them and will say a lot about you. Do not forget that the client is having an experience of you as you give the feedback, so make sure that the experience is a positive one. Take care to present the feedback in a gentle, curious, non-judgemental way that is easy for the client to hear and will not generate any defensiveness. Love is at the core of all feedback.

Coaching is sometimes about helping someone to recognise and work through their so-called 'failings', also known as 'areas for further development'! Perhaps other people describe your client as a 'bully', for example. You are offering your client an invitation to explore this behaviour and the impact it has on others. To do this, your client needs to feel safe.

Clients may well recognise their behaviour but be afraid to admit it to themselves, let alone to you. They have probably developed strong skills to camouflage this recognition, so you need to make them feel totally safe and in an environment of non-judgement where they can feel compassion for themselves. You must have total compassion, even if your client does behave in unacceptable ways.

Look for the greatness within your clients and choose to see it. When you see it, you will naturally behave towards them as if the greatness were there, and they will be able to see it and feel it in themselves through you. When clients see their greatness, they will be able to behave in ways that reveal it.

In quantum terms, you will have helped to create the resonance of greatness within your client. Their body-mind will know that this is who they really are and they will have opened up another forgotten door in their castle and stepped into their authentic being. This is the true work of the coach.

Offering feedback on the words the client uses

Since we have been looking at the energy in words, let's start with ways in which you might offer feedback to the client about the words that they use frequently, or may use typically in particular situations.

Here are some examples of words, expressions or language forms that might be worth pointing out to the client as you start to observe their speech patterns.

"I can't handle this"

When you hear the client utter this or a similar expression regularly, you may want to ask them to focus on how it feels in their body when they say it. Typically they will describe feelings ranging from or including: shrinking in size, feeling powerless, feeling energy draining out of them, feeling a downward flow of energy through their body, feeling heavy in their head or their body and sinking. Then ask them to contrast this feeling with the feeling they experience when saying "Yes, I can handle this – easily." This time the descriptions are usually something along the lines of: feeling an upward flow of energy through their body, feeling taller or straighter, feeling lighter in their head or body and starting to smile or feeling a 'smile' in their stomach area (see page 64).

When "You" means "I"

By this, I mean the client says things like "You get up exhausted in the morning and drag yourself into work" when they really mean "I get up exhausted in the morning and drag myself into work . . .", or "You get so fed up with people criticising you all the time" instead of "I get so fed up with people criticising me all the time."

Many people talk like this in second person much of the time and, when I hear them do this, I usually say something along the lines of:

> *"I notice that you often talk about 'you' instead of 'I' or 'me' when you are talking about your own experiences. My sense of the effect of this is that:*
>
>> *it can create distance between you and the person you're talking to as you do not sound as if you fully own your experiences. This prevents someone from connecting with the 'me' that does this; it may make you seem less real, more generic; and*
>>
>> *it may sound as if you assume that everyone else is the same as you, reacts in the same way as you do or wants the same things that you do. If they don't experience the same thing, this may create another barrier.*
>
> *"Now, I'm not saying that it's 'wrong' to do this, but simply that these may be the outcome of your communication and may not be giving you the results in your communication that you would like."*

"I should", "I ought to", "I must"

Many people use words of obligation like "I should", "I must", "I ought to", "I've got to" a great deal. When I hear this, I ask them how they feel when saying these words. They usually notice that they feel guilty and as if they really want to avoid doing the thing they feel they ought to do.

For example, I was talking to Dan, a team leader.

> Dan: I suppose I ought to ask the team what they think about my decision.
> Annette: How does it feel when you say you ought to?
> Dan: I feel that I don't really want to.
> Annette: What would have to happen for you to want to?

Dan: I would have to feel that they are happy with my decision. I guess I don't really want to hear what I already know – that they're not happy with it.

Then we talked about Dan's rationale for making the decision and how he might minimise the negative effects of it upon the team. Now, I am not saying that every time someone says "I ought to . . ." you would comment on this expression of obligation. This may feel to the client as if you are being nit-picking and critical. But if someone uses these expressions frequently, it can be very useful to work with this tendency.

Here is an excerpt from my conversation with Rosemary, a young manager in her late twenties.

Rosemary: I know I should feel more excited by this challenge, but somehow I don't – I feel daunted.
Annette: Who says that you should feel more excited?
Rosemary (after thinking for a minute): Me, I suppose.
Annette: Which part of 'me'?
Rosemary (after thinking again): The bit that feels I'm letting myself down, letting it down. It doesn't think I'm really good enough.

This then led us to explore Rosemary's view of herself as a competent manager, which took us down the pathway of examining the rather critical scripting she had received from her parents.

I encourage clients to be aware of their tendency to talk about obligations, to notice when they realise they are about to use these expressions and to replace them with "I will", "I want to", "I choose to", "I'm going to". The effect of this is that clients feel that they are setting themselves a target that will make them feel satisfied when they have achieved it.

"I'm worried"

Many people talk about worrying from time to time but some use this word frequently. When I hear this, I explore with them where the worrying comes from, what effect this 'W' word has upon them and any benefits the word might offer them.

Interestingly, many people say that they think they have to worry about things that are going wrong or challenging them in some way, almost as if it is a duty or a responsible thing to do. I often hear people say that if they didn't worry it might indicate that they weren't concerned enough to take the issue seriously and they wouldn't take steps to improve the situation.

As we explore the nature of worrying in this way, the client usually discovers that worrying is a depleting activity. When we tell ourselves that we are worried, it has an energy-reducing effect upon us that can suggest that we are powerless in the face of the problem, that we are not in control, leaving us less able to handle the cause of the concern. I always suggest that they eradicate the phrase "I'm worried" from their vocabulary and replace it with "I'm concerned about". The reason is that, if we tell ourselves that we are worried, we will feel worried even if we are not really. When we say "I'm concerned about it", it allows us to acknowledge the problem and generates an energy that invites us to create a strategy for solving it. Worrying is a habit and a choice and we choose it when we say "I'm worried".

"It's difficult", "I'm struggling"

Again, when I hear a client talking frequently in this way, I explore with them how it feels in their body as they talk about, for example, 'struggling'. This leads them to an understanding that using this kind of language will make them feel as if they *are* struggling and *expect* struggle in their life. 'Struggle', like 'worry' and 'should', is another word to banish from our vocabulary as the energy of the word will manifest the qualities of the word in your experience of life.

Elizabeth, a senior manager in a male-dominated organisation talked about her struggles. Whether she was talking about her boss, her children, her weight or her negative thoughts, the words 'struggle', 'hard' or 'difficult' were always in the frame.

> Annette: Where in your body do you feel the word 'struggle'?
> Elizabeth: It's a tight iron band across my chest. I'm trying to break out of it, through it, but it's constricting me – in everything.
> Annette: Try to imagine that you have burst through it, that it's shattered.
> (She visualised this for a minute, looking at first elated then terrified.)
> Annette: What's happening right now?
> Elizabeth: I'm free and strong, but I don't know what to do with it. I'm not used to feeling this way.

We spent some time exploring how much safer it felt to her to be in the familiar struggle against life's challenges than to be set free to face the unknown success and then risk failure.

"I am being accused of"

Steve, a highly driven, task-focused managing director, said this several times in our first session as he described different situations in his workplace. When I flagged this up to him, he said that he saw himself as being constantly blamed by others. This led us into a useful exploration of how he operates and his impact on others.

CHAPTER TWELVE

Offering feedback about other observations

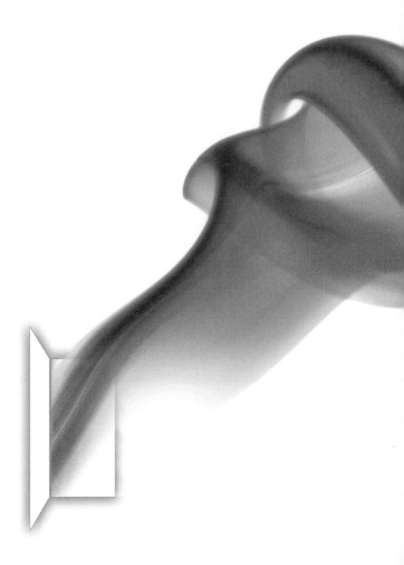

The way the client uses language is just one of the sources of holographic information available to the coach. Everything is a hologram, after all. The client is giving you, the coach, significant information about themselves in a variety of other unconscious ways, any of which, through careful feedback, can provide a valuable springboard for diving into an exploration.

Here are some further examples of the kinds of unconscious body language or behaviours that you may observe and choose to offer feedback on, which can help to identify the patterns and energy that the client is working with on a daily basis.

I tend to preface such feedback with a statement like "I am noticing that you . . .":

- "Have a tendency to frown when I ask you a question"
- "Are drumming your fingers on the table"
- "Bite your lip and breathe more loudly when we talk about your children"
- "Are perched on the edge of the chair during our sessions"
- "Curl your shoulders and wrists in"
- "Laugh when you're telling me about something unpleasant or distressing"
- "Don't smile very much".

These are all fairly typical instances of the kinds of *observable* body language or behaviours that are the doorways to useful probing. 'Observable' is the key word here.

So, as you can see, these statements are all based on what you, as the coach, have personally observed during your sessions with the client. In the last chapter, I advised:

Take care to present the feedback in a gentle, curious, non-judgemental way that is easy for the client to hear and will not generate any defensiveness. Don't forget – everything

*is information and doesn't necessarily mean what you
think or necessarily mean anything at all.*

So, here's how *not to* offer the above feedback:

"I am noticing that you . . .":

- "Have a tendency to frown when I ask you a question as if you disagree with me"
- "Are drumming your fingers on the table impatiently"
- "Bite your lip nervously and breathe more loudly when we talk about your children"
- "Are perched on the edge of the chair during our sessions as if you are uncomfortable"
- "Curl your shoulders and wrists in like a nervous kitten"
- "Laugh inappropriately when you're telling me about something unpleasant or distressing"
- "Look serious most of the time and don't smile very much".

As you can see, the additions imply a judgement, suggest that they should not be doing these things and may therefore induce defensiveness. Though I am not going to examine each of these statements and give worked examples of the possible avenues of exploration that may result from such feedback, the last two examples are worth looking at in more detail.

"I notice that you laugh when you're telling me about something unpleasant or distressing"

This is a recognisable and commonplace reaction that some people have to talking about their personal difficulties. They utter a spontaneous little burst of laughter often accompanied by a tight or wry smile. It is often called 'inappropriate laughter' and can represent a number of different internal responses to the statement, such as "Poor me, look at what I'm coping with"; "See how brave I'm being"; "Well what else can I expect? Life always treats me like this"; "They're to blame as usual"; "They always mess things up like this"; "Life's a bitch and then you die."

These examples of the client's possible internal commentary are all useful avenues to explore as they will offer real insights into their view of the world and their limiting beliefs about themselves or how things work. They would have to be articulated by the client and not suggested by the coach as this would either feel like a judgement or make them feel that they were being led by the coach.

However, I would mention once again that if you are familiar with the term 'inappropriate laughter' do not name this behaviour as such. It is on the list of 'how not to give feedback' because it is an example of labelling instead of making an observation.

"I notice that you don't smile very much"

Smiling is one of the most significant aspects of interpersonal interactions in our western culture. Its effect is to relax other people and make them feel listened to as well as to relax yourself. It is not the same in most eastern or Asian cultures, so this feedback would not be appropriate to offer to a client from these cultures.

Again, I am not suggesting that it is wrong not to smile much, but it does tend to create outcomes in interactions and relationships that detract from, rather than enhance, them. So, when coaching a client whose goal is to improve their ability to create strong personal relationships or improve their personal impact on others, and you observe that they smile infrequently, it is relevant to work on this.

Typically, after giving the client feedback about not smiling a great deal and exploring the issue further with them, I usually suggest that they try the following exercise (The smile survey) for homework, which will enable them to draw their own conclusions about the effects of smiling. My experience is that a great many (but by no means all) of those who smile infrequently are highly cognitive, task-focused, logical-minded individuals who tend to value the process of the mind rather than that of the heart. This is an extreme generalisation, and there are also a great many other types of 'non-smiley' people around. However, because this former group would have a greater tendency to regard some form of smiling exercise as woolly, flaky or illogical, I have designed the exercise in the form of a semi-scientific survey to appeal to their cognitive nature.

The insights that the clients gain from the experiment range from mildly interesting to staggering, so I offer it here to you for use with your clients. Sometimes I have occasion to meet the spouses or partners of my clients, and they often ask me "What on earth did you do to change him/her so much?" I refute that I have done any changing, but am convinced that this simple smile survey has contributed massively to the behavioural change in their loved one.

The smile survey

Ask your client to conduct a semi-scientific survey as follows, keeping notes of their observations in a small notebook. A central premise of the survey is based upon their use of their awareness muscle (see items marked *), so you will need to have previously introduced them to this concept.

- Observe how you feel, emotionally and in your body* when others smile/don't smile at you when talking to you.
- How do you feel* when you smile/don't smile when talking to others?
- How do you observe others behaving or responding when you smile/don't smile?

- How do others seem to respond to you when you smile/don't smile when on the telephone?
- Watch how often people smile when on the telephone.
- See if you can tell whether people you're talking to on the phone are smiling or not. How does this make you feel?*
- If you are talking on the phone to someone who you think is not smiling, see if you can make them smile.
- Experiment, observe and explore all this in a semi-scientific way.
- Smile fifteen times a day for no particular reason. This does not mean you have to go about with an inane grin on your face all the time even when it would not be appropriate. It means breaking into a genuine smile, which involves your eyes (a smile that doesn't involve the eyes is a scary thing to behold!) in appropriate situations in which you would not normally smile.

Simple as this exercise is, the results can be truly astounding for someone who has not been in the habit of smiling much until then. After a couple of weeks of conducting this survey, people find that others smile at them, talk to them and include them more, and they feel happier and more relaxed than they have ever been.

The value of developing a ready smile is demonstrated in Malcolm Gladwell's book *Blink*, where he describes a study conducted by a team of German psychologists. They showed cartoons to a group of subjects each of whom was holding a pen in their mouth. Some had the pen between their teeth and the others between their lips. When you hold a pen between your lips, it is impossible to smile, as you are physically unable to contract either of the two major smiling muscles (the risorius and the zygomatic major). Holding a pen between your teeth has the opposite effect and forces you to smile (though not with the eyes!)

So, what happened? Well, believe it or not, the study showed that the people with the pen between their teeth found the cartoons much funnier. We tend to assume that we have to experience an emotion first for it to be expressed on our face, that the face is where emotions are revealed. This is only partly true: making an expression can also create the emotion. So you can 'fake it 'til you make it' and create the emotion you want. This is what is at the heart of great acting. And if simply holding your mouth in a false smile like this results in your seeing things in a more light-hearted way, think what happens when you are really smiling with your eyes and whole body. It also makes perfect sense if we look at this from a quantum physics point of view. Everything is connected, the facial muscles and the smile are connected to every other part of the body – every organ and every cell. When you smile, your whole body smiles.

In a film some time ago, Anthony Hopkins was playing the part of a man who had a heart attack. He refused to rehearse the scene more than once because he felt his heart and body mirrored the symptoms of cardiac arrest as he acted out the scene, and he did not want to subject his body to any unnecessary risk.

More on feedback

Having offered you some rules for giving feedback to the client earlier in this chapter, I will now show you some examples in which I may seem to violate them. This just goes to show that there are no ultimate rules, just guidelines.

There are times when, if you feel it would be useful for the client to get a really clear sense of what you are observing, you might choose to say what the behaviour reminds you of. But take care to choose a simile that shows compassion, not judgement. It is a powerful statement and the client will remember the simile long afterwards. As I mentioned earlier, one of the holographic aspects of the way people present themselves is the extent to which they give a sense of being fully in their power. Feeling 'less than' others in some areas of our life can lead to giving away our power. When we are in our full power, we do not give it away but give off the sense of feeling confident and happy with ourselves and strong in our identity. People give their power away through, for example, their breathing, speech patterns and use of their voice.

Here is an example using a simile in giving feedback to a client who seemed to be giving away his power.

Case Study Two

A middle manager, Phil, had just moved into a new post where a major skill required of him would be the ability to articulate an argument effectively and be able to influence others to follow his recommendations. He sought coaching to develop his style of communication and influencing. I explored with him what he felt was the essence of being influential and as he spoke I observed that he did not seem to be fully 'standing in his power'. The way he talked, very rapidly and almost skimming across the top of what he wanted to say without really getting into the words, gave me a sense that this might be a way in which he was giving away some of his power.

I asked him if I could give him my observation of his communication style and he agreed.

> Annette: I feel that you have a lightness around you rather like a dragonfly or daddy-long-legs. Your energy seems to be flitting around and doesn't seem to be totally grounded, which gives me an impression that you don't seem to be 'present'.
> Phil: Yes, I'm often more in the future than the present.
> Annette: (Observing how Phil seemed to project his voice.) Your breath and speech seem to emanate from your

head area rather than from deeper down in your body. Your words seem to flutter into your head and out of your mouth. Because your voice seems to come from your head, neck and throat rather than your belly, the effect is that your energy is not centred in yourself or grounded. This might be working against you.

As you see, I used similes here to give Phil a visual picture of my observations, which he accepted and expressed a willingness to work with. The rule of feedback 'being for the benefit of the other person' is paramount. Everything you say to clients and the way you say it should make them feel that you are totally 'in their corner' and have no judgement about them, even as you are offering feedback about ways in which their impact may not be serving them.

Phil worked very hard with me over about six months and he learned to draw his energy from a place deeper inside of himself and speak from that place, more slowly and in a focused way that made others want to listen to his words. I spoke to Phil recently on the telephone several years after his coaching programme finished and could hear that his energy was still grounded and his communication focused. I commented that he seemed to be truly 'in his power' and he confirmed that he had been feeling this way ever since our coaching programme.

Feedback as a pointer to an underlying issue

Because you are giving non-evaluative feedback, in other words flagging up the behaviour rather than an assessment of what the behaviour means, you are leaving the space open for a true exploration. Within this space, results ranging from interesting to minor miracles can emerge. Here is an example of an interesting revelation.

Case Study Three

I was coaching Martina, a middle manager, on improving her
self-presentation and communication skills. Rather like Phil in
the previous example, after a couple of sessions, through
feedback from me leading to further exploration, we identified
poor concentration and a lack of focus in Martina's
communication as being an area for development. At one
point during our third session when I was saying something,
she seemed to lose her concentration, so I flagged this up for
her.

Annette: I noticed that you seemed to 'switch off' for a
minute or two just now. This is something that I see you
do quite often.

Martina: Yes, I noticed it too just then, and I know it's
something I do pretty often as well. My concentration
goes.

Annette: So, tell me what happens when your concentration
goes while you're talking to people.

Martina: Maybe my eyes move or I look away from their
eyes. Or perhaps something they say hooks me onto a
train of thought away from what they're saying.

Annette: What kind of train of thought?

Martina: It might be a memory about something. Or it could
be an idea that just comes to me. Sometimes it might be
that I start thinking about something that's happened to
me.

Annette: So you stop listening because you start thinking?

Martina: Yes, I sort of wander off.

Annette: What do you think might trigger this 'wandering
off mode'?

Martina: All the work waiting for me on my desk, crowding
into my brain from behind.

Annette: Can you try, right now, to focus on the 'work-load
thoughts' moving into your brain?

Martina: Ok. Yes they're there now.

Annette: What do you think they are feeling and thinking about you?

Martina: They're thinking "Let's distract her. Let's sit on the wall and jump down and distract her while she's talking."

Annette: Why would they need to do this?

Martina: To get attention.

Annette: And why would they need to get attention?

Martina: They feel left out, as if they're not getting enough attention. They're afraid of not being dealt with. They're thinking "I'm not important enough to get her attention."

Annette: This sounds a bit like little children trying to get noticed.

Martina: They're like little green blobs jumping up and down, crying "Please take *me*, make it *me*."

Annette: What would the little green blobs need to make them sit quietly on your desk and wait patiently for you to get to them?"

Martina: (Laughing.) A video.

Annette: What would a video do for them?

Martina: Keep them entertained and distracted, happy and contented.

Annette: Is there anything they could do for themselves while they're waiting? What work could they do on their own?

Martina: They might chug away at finding solutions for themselves if they were happy and if they thought that they were important to me.

Annette: How could you let them know that they are important to you?

Martina: Write them down.

Annette: Do you usually write them down?

Martina: No, hardly ever.

So, out of this piece of feedback about Martina's apparent lapse of attention has emerged another issue to which she needs to pay attention – time management. Her lack of time management skills is contributing to her lack of concentration and affecting her communication with others. The crucial thing here was that I did not make any assumptions about what was happening when I saw her attention wander, and this created space for the real issue to emerge. Martina's lack of time management skills was not the 'answer' to her ineffective communication but it was certainly a contributing factor. We spent the rest of the session looking further at Martina's time management system, or lack of it.

Since effective time management is core to personal effectiveness, I am always alert to the possibility that people who are not getting the results that they want in their life do not have an effective time management system in place, either at work or in their personal lives. I believe that if a person cannot describe their time management system they do not have one. Whenever a client alludes to struggling in this area of their life, I offer them a practical tool from the tool kit to help them. Although I do not cover the topic of time management thoroughly in this book, I will recommend to you a great tool that I offer my clients, which you may have already met. It is from Stephen Covey's renowned book *The Seven Habits of Highly Effective People* and is what he calls the 'Quadrant II' system.

(Although not concerned with quantum ideas, the Quadrant II tool is, in my view, an essential basic tool kit item for all coaches.)

Many people are nervous of adopting a time management system for fear that it will constrict them and they will have to organise their lives around the 'system', which will not allow them to live life to the full and be spontaneous. Covey's system is just the opposite of this. It is designed to enable people to achieve the important, life-affirming actions that bring about the realisation of their dreams and potential while at the same time getting the routine, run-of-the-mill tasks, like tax returns, completed effortlessly before they grow fangs and turn into problems.

Analysis of the case study

Let's have another look at Case Study Three and pick out the moments where I made an intuitive, quantum leap in my questioning. Remember, the quantum leap question is one that leads to a series of fruitful insights.

> Annette: I noticed that you seemed to 'switch off' for a minute or two just now. This is something that I see you do quite often.
>
> Martina: Yes, I noticed it too just then, and I know it's something I do pretty often as well. My concentration goes.
>
> Annette: So, tell me what happens when your concentration goes while you're talking to people.
>
> Martina: Maybe my eyes move or I look away from their eyes. Or perhaps something they say hooks me onto a train of thought away from what they're saying.
>
> Annette: What kind of train of thought?
>
> **(In both of my questions so far I have used exactly the same words that the client uses.)**
>
> Martina: It might be a memory about something. Or it could be an idea that just comes to me. Sometimes it might be that I start thinking about something that's happened to me.
>
> Annette: So you stop listening because you start thinking?
>
> **(Summarising what she is saying in my own words to check out with her that I have got the picture.)**
>
> Martina: Yes, I sort of wander off.
>
> Annette: What do you think might trigger this 'wandering off mode'?
>
> **(Now that we have clarified what is physically happening and summarised it, it's time to explore what is causing it, using Martina's words. If I used my own words, 'wandering off' may sound like a judgement.)**
>
> Martina: All the work waiting for me on my desk, crowding into my brain from behind.

Annette: Can you try, right now, to focus on the 'work-load thoughts' moving into your brain?
(Inviting her to go into the body-mind and feel what's happening.)

Martina: OK. Yes, they're there now.

Annette: What do you think they are feeling and thinking about you?
(This might look like a quantum leap question but is actually a fairly typical quantum skills question. As in Michael's case study with the red blob, it is often very instructive to personify the feeling and explore the relationship between this personified 'feeling-being' and the client. Asking what the feeling-being might think or feel about the client is a good way to do this. It often gives the client fresh insights into how she treats and relates to herself.)

Martina: They're thinking "Let's distract her. Let's sit on the wall and jump down and distract her while she's talking.
(It's quite fun for the client to do and because it's not a predictable, cognitive avenue of exploration the answers come straight from the body-mind – spontaneous and authentic.)

Annette: Why would they need to do this?
(In the same way that everything that people do has a pay-off of some kind, we treat the personalised feeling-being as if it were a person and try to identify the pay-offs of its behaviours. And, of course, it *is* a person, it is a part of the client.)

Martina: To get attention.

Annette: And why would they need to get attention?

Martina: They feel left out, as if they're not getting enough attention. They're afraid of not being dealt with. They're thinking "I'm not important enough to get her attention."

Annette: This sounds a bit like little children trying to get noticed.
(This is a quantum leap statement based on the way the feeling-beings are expressing themselves. It sounds to me like the way children talk, so I allow my intuition to speak.)

Martina: They're like little green blobs jumping up and down, crying "Please take *me*, make it *me*."

Annette: What would the little green blobs need to make them sit quietly on your desk and wait patiently for you to get to them?"

(Continuing the theme of the feeling-beings being like children.)

Martina: (Laughing.) A video.

Annette: What would a video do for them?

Martina: Keep them entertained and distracted, happy and contented.

(Even though it seemed fairly obvious that this would be the answer, I prefer to ask the client and let her say it than for me to state this assumption or even just think it. Having it articulated in this way by the client allows me to use it as the springboard for the next question.)

Annette: Is there anything they could do for themselves while they're waiting? What work could they do on their own?

(Moving towards problem solving.)

Martina: They might chug away at finding solutions for themselves if they were happy and if they thought that they were important to me.

Annette: How could you let them know that they are important to you?

(Following up on the client's insights into what the feeling-beings need. This is another example of the exploration helping to integrate the client with the feeling-beings she is working with.)

Martina: Write them down.

Annette: Do you usually write them down?

Martina: No, hardly ever.

CHAPTER THIRTEEN

Feedback about the impact of the client's behaviour upon you

I have mentioned that feedback on your observations of the client's behaviour can sometimes extend to your describing its effect upon you. Why is this relevant? At the beginning of Chapter Eleven, we said that the last thing we discover about ourselves is our impact on others. People who have a negative impact upon others rarely receive constructive feedback about their behaviour. People might tell them what they think of them in an accusing way but not with compassion or a desire to help them to step into their greatness. And yet this is the feedback they most need to receive. They need to hear how they affect others from someone who accepts them (you can accept another person without approving of their behaviour), cares about them and wants nothing more than to see them become the finest version of themselves that they can be. They need to feel safe as they hear it. This is why it is so important that the coach is able to offer this feedback when necessary.

'HPLR' is my own term for highly task-focused individuals who get great results in the workplace but do so in a way that leaves other people feeling demeaned, disrespected or generally disregarded. HPLR means High Performance, Low Relationship. We all know them. They drive forward towards the goal demolishing all barriers in the way and get outstanding results. When criticised because some of the barriers are human ones and folk get hurt in the process, they say things like "Well, you can't argue with my success. Look at what I achieve", or "I'm paid to get the job done and I do just that. I'm not paid to worry about other people's feelings." The You Can't Argue With My Success syndrome usually shuts people up into a resentful silence, but the feelings do not go away. *People will always forget what you did. People will always forget what you said. But people will never forget how you made them feel.*

But, if you remember in the list of rules for giving feedback, rule 7 was "Remember that a fault is simply an overuse of a quality." So, what qualities is the HPLR overusing? Enthusiasm for doing the job well; a high level of energy and competence; a drive for results; being a hard worker; loyalty to the chain of command; rising above their own emotional needs.

Case Study Four

A few years ago, I was asked to coach Tony, a very senior director and an entrenched member of the HPLR school of management! It was Tony's boss who made this request. I began the process by conducting a 360 degree feedback process on Tony,[5] which showed clearly that he was indeed an HPLR: he paid great attention to the task but showed scant regard for his staff. Although he achieved consistently good results, he was, at that time, also facing harassment charges against him for his overly robust treatment of one of his team members.

I arranged a meeting with him to show him the results of his 360 report and discuss how he wanted to proceed. Not surprisingly, he received me with a look of withering contempt as if to say he would have no difficulty in intimidating this pink and fluffy lightweight consultant. However, I had decided before even meeting him that I would look for his qualities even if he made every effort to conceal them. As I talked to him, I saw a very shy, diffident man brandishing a glinting shield of aggressiveness as a protection. The power that this offered him did not quite obscure the hint of sadness and mischief in his face. He was highly competent at his job and had a strong drive to achieve a great output.

When I presented his feedback report, he did not seem remotely phased by it and started by articulating the standard HPLR strap-line.

---

5. 360 degree feedback is where an individual receives feedback from all those around them (hence 360 degrees). The boss, direct reports and peers all complete questionnaires about their experience of working with the individual, who is also invited to complete a questionnaire about their own perception of their personal impact and working style.

Tony: Just look at what I achieve! I'm paid to get the job done and I do just that, thank you very much. I'm not paid to worry about other people's feelings.

Annette: **(I knew I was in for a challenge!)** My definition of leadership is 'getting results through others'. Management is not leadership. Management is getting involved with the processes and procedures. But as a leader, the results that your team or department achieves are your results. The better they perform, the better you perform. As a leader, you need to really listen to your people and learn what they need so you can give them what they need to work their best for you.

Tony: (Leaning back in his chair, and with a sardonic tone.) So tell me, do you think I'm listening to you right now?

Annette: Technically speaking, you probably are: your eyes are towards me and you're not covering up your ears. All the same, I don't feel that you're really listening. I can see that all the tiny muscles around your eyes and mouth look tight, your facial colouration is quite high, you seem to be breathing quite rapidly from your upper chest and you're tapping your thumb on the desk. I feel that all these things going on in your body language are giving me the message 'Get on with it woman!'

Tony: Yes, that's exactly what I am thinking!

Annette: Well, Tony, I know that I'm good at my job, but right now your body language is making me feel uneasy and slightly anxious. If I were working for you, I know I would not be working at my best. You wouldn't be getting the best performance out of me. Now, I want you to know that I'm not telling you this so that you should feel sorry for me. I'm telling you because if I feel this way then it's quite likely that other people do too. And your 360 results seem to indicate that they do. Since leadership is getting results through others, you may think you're getting great results, but I believe that you could get even better results if you paid more attention to your staff.

(As I was saying this, Tony visibly and unexpectedly shifted into listening mode and his whole demeanour changed, just for a nano-second.)

Annette: But right now you are listening. I can see it. Your face has softened, the muscles around your eyes and mouth, have relaxed, your facial colouring has reduced, and it feels like you're interested in what I'm saying. You're giving off a supporting feeling right now.

(The fact that it was so immediately obvious to me that he had switched into listening mode seemed to unnerve him somewhat. In his own body, he could feel that he had made this shift, but he was totally unaware of the effect this might have on someone else.)

Annette: If I were working for you when you're in this mode, I would feel relaxed and confident. I would feel that I wanted to do my best for you and would undoubtedly produce much higher-quality work as a result.

(At one point towards the end of the session, I 'switched off' momentarily while he was talking, as I became aware of needing to bring the session to a close and establish some action points. He instantly spotted this and knew that I wasn't listening.)

Tony: (Jubilantly.) Ha! And now you're not listening *to me*!

Annette: Yes, I'm sorry I did switch off for a moment. How did this make you feel?

Tony: I felt ignored, annoyed actually. It wasn't respectful.

Annette: This is what your 360 is saying about how you make people feel most of the time. People are not feeling respected by you. And it is almost certainly affecting their performance and how willing they are to go the extra mile for you in a crisis.

This did the trick! He realised that what I was saying was true, because I was mirroring back to him what he did to other people. What's more, he could feel in his own body firstly that he was listening when I pointed it out and secondly that he felt ignored and disrespected when I switched off.

Tony agreed to continue with more coaching sessions and within six weeks he was a changed man. He worked hard and courageously to challenge his beliefs about the world, other people and himself as we explored and worked through the underlying cause of his lack of concern for others. Within a few weeks, the senior members of his department were approaching him individually and were saying "We're all working better these days because you've changed!" And they requested that they also be offered the chance to experience the same coaching process that he had undergone.

I have described Tony's case study in some detail, as it is a fairly typical example of situations in which this type of quite personal feedback is valuable. I have worked in this way on a number of occasions, always with a positive outcome. The single most crucial aspect of being able to carry it off effectively is that the coach is genuinely in the client's corner – seeing and believing totally in their greatness and genuinely wanting to help them step into it.

When not to give feedback or coaching

I would just like to offer you some words of caution on giving feedback about behaviour, and coaching in general.

- Friends and family will ask you to coach them from time to time. Of course, it is a pleasure to be able to talk a loved one through a troublesome situation and this may involve giving them feedback. You will feel the certain shift in role as you coach them: the friendship or family relationship is still at the root of the conversation, but because you are in 'coaching mode' it feels different for the duration of the conversation. It is as if you step out of the usual arena of the friendship and into the coaching 'space'. Afterwards, we step back into the friendship. It is not that the friendship is not there during the coaching, just that the nature of the interaction is very different from the kind of interaction that you would normally have in the friendship.

■ Just because you know that they value your coaching questions and insightful feedback when they ask you for it, do not assume that they want it whenever (what appears to you) a great coaching opportunity pops up. Try to restrain yourself from going into 'coaching mode' unless they ask you specifically. They may feel irritated by this and not want to tell you for fear of hurting your feelings.

■ If someone other than a client asks you for feedback, think very carefully before agreeing, be it a friend or anyone else. Beware – even if you check out with them why they are asking you and they reply that they are open to learning whatever they can to help them to become more effective, communicative, positive and so on, it might not quite work out like that. The coaching relationship is a three-way interaction: the coach, the client and the coaching relationship. It is the relationship that grants the coach the right to challenge the client, take them out of their comfort zone and offer them feedback. Without the context of the coaching relationship, any feedback you give may be appreciated at the time, but, if it is at all challenging, it is highly likely that the person will quickly resent it, and you.

CHAPTER FOURTEEN

How coaching outcomes are affected by the coach's beliefs

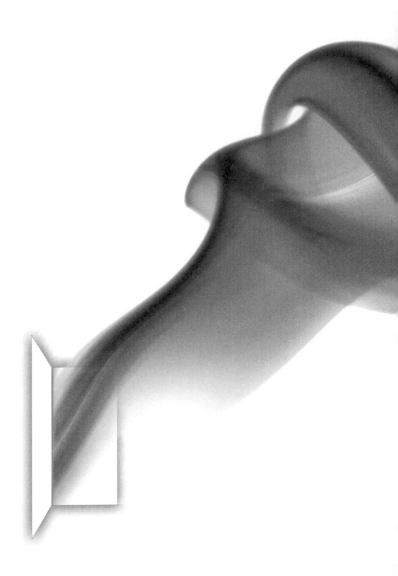

You are probably getting the idea now that everything is energy! Words, thoughts, intentions, beliefs – everything. We have been talking a lot about how to help clients choose beliefs that will serve rather than impede their lives by raising their awareness of how beliefs transmit themselves through the quantum soup, affecting outcomes all around them. In exactly the same way, the beliefs that the coach holds will affect the coaching process, and we need to examine our beliefs about our clients just as we examine our intent when giving them feedback. In the case studies in the last chapter, we can clearly see the vital role played by a 'pure intent' in giving any kind of feedback, particularly in Case Study Four with Tony.

Choosing to see clients as whole, healthy and good, and to accept them for who they are without judgement, is crucial to your work with them. This choice is a belief. Even if you do not agree with or support their beliefs or behaviour patterns, you can choose to see the goodness in them. If you do not, you cannot coach them effectively. When you accept someone as a coaching client, you owe it to them to adopt positive beliefs. If you feel that you cannot do this, do not accept the person as a client. A belief such as this one is a keystone belief for the coach to hold. It is a bedrock belief that underpins transformational coaching, without which the coaching cannot succeed.

Another keystone belief that I hold about the human condition is that, generally speaking, *good health and happiness are our 'default settings' as human beings.* They are our birthright, our natural way of being. I say 'generally speaking' here because there are certain mysteries about life and death that we cannot fathom; that is why they are mysteries. To say that our bodies and minds will always try to attain these default settings is somewhat simplistic and is to deny this mystery, which may sometimes mean that a living system develops an illness for no apparent reason. Many spiritual teachers die of cancer, for example.

Sometimes such great learning emerges from within the suffering or illness that these things become a blessing. As Eckhart Tolle says:

> "Life will give you whatever experience is most helpful for the evolution of your consciousness. How do you know this is the experience you need? Because it's the experience you're having at this moment."

Larry Dossey explores this issue in great depth in his book *Healing Words*, concluding that we have to be willing to stand in the unknown. He quotes Gertrude Stein:

> "A PAINLESS PATH
> There is no answer
> There never has been an answer
> There never will be an answer
> That's the answer."

Nevertheless, I still feel that it is helpful for coaches, while holding this unknowable mystery in their hearts, to practise coaching as if it were true that health and happiness are our default settings. Why? Because it helps the client for you to believe this.

So let's say that our bodies and minds will *almost always* try to attain these default settings in the same way that living systems will try to achieve homeostasis (or equilibrium) and water will always try to reach its own level. There is what seems to be an inner intelligence at work tirelessly pushing the system towards good health and happiness. Provide the physical body with the right conditions, nutritious diet, sufficient exercise, healthy thought processes, a nourishing environment, appropriate medication and so on and it will usually remain healthy or heal itself. As healers and doctors know, all healing is ultimately self-healing and happens when the conditions are conducive to good health.

In the same way, create the right conditions and a person will be happy or move towards achieving happiness. If you ask people "What do you want in life?" or "What do you want for your children?", most will answer "To be happy" and "For them to be happy." This ceaseless striving for happiness is built into our systems, although many people do not recognise if they are happy or not. But they do know if they are not happy, even if they do not think about it consciously.

At the beginning of this book, I told the story of the child rediscovering the hidden rooms in her castle; you might see a link here. When we begin to rediscover our true selves by walking through the doors of these rooms, we start to regain a sense of who we are, which is a thrilling thing to experience. It leads us towards becoming the finest version of ourselves that we can be and involves learning new skills, reframing our assumptions about how we fit into the world and opening ourselves up to new experiences and emotions. It also leads to increased levels of happiness. Just as we have an inbuilt drive to attain happiness, I believe that we have a similar drive to become the finest version of ourselves that we can be. When we get our first taste of this, it helps create the happiness we strive for. So another of the essential key beliefs for the coach to hold is that each client has this inner drive at work pushing them towards being the finest version of themselves they can be. They may not know this and may even be behaving in ways that proclaim "I don't care about it", but if you believe it to be true then you will coach them accordingly, and ultimately help to show them their greatest gifts.

In other words, the coaching process benefits from coaches who hold the belief that happiness is our default setting, and the reason for this is that it helps you to work with people who appear to have a very external focus and those we might refer to as HPLRs. Even if someone is behaving in a way that looks pretty inappropriate, aggressive, unconnected with others or cut off from the world, remembering that this person basically wants to be happy and probably is not will enable you to feel compassion and to work with them in such a way that you can flag this up energetically. You don't need to talk about happiness; this might feel like an invasion of privacy and would probably make the client run a mile. Just feeling for someone, sensing that on the happiness scale they might score two or three out of ten and knowing that their inner self craves their own happiness, is enough to shape your questions and your approach.

Eckhart Tolle says:

> *"When we come into the presence of someone who truly accepts us for who we are, the healing begins."*

A coach is not a healer, you might say. In Chapter Three, we saw that coaching is not therapy but it can be experienced as being very therapeutic. Coaching is not healing either, yet it can bring about a tremendous healing of emotional pain and the underlying issues that caused it. Being in the presence of someone who truly accepts you, does not judge you or label your behaviours, can create the soul-nourishing conditions that are conducive to inner healing. If that person is your coach, their coaching will be healing to you and can contribute to your moving towards the happiness that is your birthright.

CHAPTER FIFTEEN

Intuition

What is intuition? Perhaps a look at some dictionary definitions is a good place to start:

- The state of being aware of or knowing something without having to discover or perceive it, or the ability to do this
- Something known or believed instinctively, without actual evidence for it
- Immediate knowledge of something.

Recently both the light and ceiling fan in our kitchen stopped working for no obvious reason. My husband and I tried all the usual problem-solving, eliminating-the-possible-causes type investigations to work it out (checking the bulbs and all the other electrical sockets and appliances in the room) but we could not isolate the problem. During this process, the merest whisper of an idea to check out a third switch on the other side of the wall to the two switches shimmered in and out of my head. Before I had even realised it, the thought had gone. My husband then spent the next few hours on a trip to the hardware store to buy two (quite expensive) dimmer switches and then wiring them in, but still no joy. The problem remained. The next morning, while using the socket on the other side of the wall, the kitchen lights and ceiling fan came on. Darn it! If only I had listened to that little whisper to check out that master socket! It happens all the time, doesn't it? Sometimes we do catch the thought that shimmers in and out of our head in time to pay attention to it, and sometimes we don't.

That is what intuition is. And, like everything else, it is an energy form! It is the "knowing that doesn't know that it knows" that nudges you at the moment you need to pay attention to it. This knowing is nothing to do with facts that we 'know' or concepts which we understand, or theories we have worked out. It is not even a thought that says "What if . . .?" It is an energetic vibration that flickers light on the knowing for a nano-moment. It is similar to the awareness muscle in several ways:

- It is something that most people do not pay attention to, until we realise that the information in this flickering is useful
- We find that we can learn to recognise the sensation of it within the energy system of our body and become increasingly familiar with it
- We all experience these energetic nudges. (Some people might claim that they do not, and this is just because they have not yet attuned their antennae finely enough to pick up the resonance. We can all learn to do this.)

You will find, as you become familiar with the quantum tools and use them more frequently, that you will automatically start to recognise your intuition whispering. Just using the tools will serve as an exercise to start to develop your intuitive awareness. The more you start to notice, pay attention to and act on the way it nudges you, the more you will find yourself saying "What a good thing I listened to myself in this situation!" and be encouraged to continue to do so. Even so, there will still be times when you fail to notice the fleeting prompts and ignore the hunch to check on that switch on the wall! And the learning there is even more pronounced as you say "If only I had listened to myself!" It is the same process as learning to pay attention to your awareness muscle. In fact it's just another aspect of the awareness muscle.

In the case studies we have looked at so far (pp. 112, 115, 163), I indicated the moments when I made an intuitive leap, or quantum leap, in the coaching session. I would suggest that you spend a few minutes now revisiting these before we look at the subject of intuition a bit more closely in the next case study.

Case Study Five

Lynne, a confident, single, childless entrepreneur in her mid-thirties, had a fear of driving on the motorway and came to me to see if coaching might help to shift it. Agreeing to work with a client on a phobia such as this is unusual for a coach as it obviously strays into the arena of therapy. She understood that coaching is not therapy but asked me to do this anyway as she had heard that the way I work was unusual and had the potential to address deeply embedded issues. I agreed because I was interested to see if indeed the quantum tools would be useful in such an instance, and because I honoured the trust she was showing in making the request, particularly since she already suspected that the causes for the phobia might be deep-veined.

I began the session by talking to her about the whole context of the issue of her experience with motorway driving. She said that it feels as if the lanes of the motorway were within 'motorway walls', which close in on her as she drives, making her feel trapped and enclosed by them. In this initial exploration of the overall context of this phobia, we found that it embraced a number of other issues in her life:

- A mental breakdown that she had suffered a few years previously during which a number of life issues surfaced
- Her feelings about her physicality and sexuality
- Her emotions around abandonment and failure – she was adopted as a child and felt abandoned by her birth mother and father
- Her experiences with therapy.

    Annette: When you think of driving on the motorway, whereabouts in your body do you experience the feelings?

    Lynne: They're in my head.

    (I asked the focusing questions separately about their colour, texture, noise and so on.)

Lynne: They're red, shiny and spiky. They're kind of
  overwhelming. And the noise they're making sounds
  like an oncoming tidal wave. It's as if they're on the
  other side of a dyke.

Annette: Who built the dyke?

Lynne: I did. The feelings are emotions of abandonment,
  fear and failure, and of not being good enough or
  wanted.

Annette: Is there any little chink in the dyke that you
  could find?

Lynne: Yes, there is one.

Annette: Could you creep through the chink so that you
  can be with them?

Lynne: (This was *really difficult* for her.) It feels as if they
  will overpower me – perhaps eat me – devour me. I'm
  not big enough to keep them at bay.

Annette: What are they saying that they want you to
  hear?

Lynne: "We want peace."

Annette: How could you give this to them?

Lynne: I don't know how to.

Annette: Is there anything that you want to say to them?

Lynne: Yes. "Leave me alone!"

Annette: Do they know who you are?

Lynne: No.

Annette: Who are you to them?

Lynne: Their mother.

Annette: Can you tell them this?

Lynne: Yes. I really want to give them the peace they ask
  for but I don't know how. I also want them to go
  away.

Annette: Does this mean putting them up for adoption?

Lynne: (She whispered.) I don't know.

Annette: Perhaps you might let them take what they
  need from you?

Lynne: I'm afraid that they'd eat me.

> Annette: What nourishment are they seeking from you by eating you?
>
> Lynne: Peace.
>
> Annette: If they are your children and you their mother, perhaps you might want to give them what they need so badly?
>
> Annette: All right, I'll try. I'll let them come to me. (This was *extremely courageous* as she was quite frightened here.)
>
> Lynne: I can feel them coming into me through my stomach. This is weird, I can actually feel them, physically inside me, kind of thrashing around. (She experienced this for a moment or two.) And now they've suddenly turned into a handful of little fishlike things. Now, they're swimming off – inside of me. They seem to be comfortable now, inside me.

At this point she looked peaceful and comfortable, as if she had returned from an eventful journey. We both knew that this was the appropriate place to stop. Peace seemed to be a theme in this journey and it seemed that once the feeling-beings were peaceful, so was she. After this session, Lynne was able to drive on the motorway, tentatively at first but with no physical or emotional symptoms. And then after a short while was able to do so with full confidence.

Before we analyse this case study, you might like to, as an exercise, study it on your own for five minutes or so. Try to get into the mood of this session, get a sense of Lynne's fear as the exploration deepened, pick out the intuitive leap questions, get a feeling for how they came to me and how, in this potentially quite traumatic session, I tried to keep her safe while at the same time helping her to move towards a healing as well as a useful outcome. You may also have questions as to why I followed a particular pathway of questioning rather than an alternative pathway that you feel might have been fruitful.

Analysis of the case study

Annette: When you think of driving on the motorway,
whereabouts in your body do you experience the
feelings?

(The, by now familiar to you, focusing questions.)

Lynne: They're in my head.

**(I asked the focusing questions separately about their colour,
texture, noise and so on.)**

Lynne: They're red, shiny and spiky. They're kind of
overwhelming. And the noise they're making sounds like
an oncoming tidal wave. It's as if they're on the other
side of a dyke.

**(There's quite a lot of information here and you might have
wondered why I chose to ask the next question about the
dyke rather than the characteristics of the feelings or the noise
they make. 'Red, shiny and spiky': I do not believe that these
factors are particularly significant. As I said earlier, the reason
for asking focusing questions is to give the client a handle on
the feelings so that she can visualise them. '. . . sounds like
an oncoming tidal wave' – yes, this is an interesting
description, but I was more curious to find out about the dyke.
If I had gone down the tidal wave route, I do believe that
somehow the pathway of the exploration would have led us to
a similar outcome.)**

Annette: Who built the dyke?

**(The question is about exploring the characteristics of the
dyke, a central characteristic of which is that someone made it
– someone must have put it there and I wondered who.)**

Lynne: I did. The feelings are emotions of abandonment,
fear and failure, and of not being good enough or
wanted.

**(You might wonder why my next question was not about her
description of these powerful emotions. As in the previous
example of the tidal wave, there is no 'right' question to ask at
any one point in an exploration. If I had asked about the
emotions, the pathway of the session may or may not have**

been quite different. But when, as the coach, you are aligned with the energy of the issue and with the client, you will always find the right question to ask.)

Annette: Is there any little chink in the dyke that you could find?

(This closed question might look like a leading one, but it didn't feel like it to me. When I asked Lynne who built the dyke, the answer felt significant and I did not want to waste it by not following up on it. I might have asked a variety of other questions about the building of it: what she wanted to achieve by building it or about how she was feeling while building it and so on. But, hey, there is no one 'right question'! Any of the other possibilities might have led us to an equally useful outcome, or to the same outcome from a different direction.)

Lynne: Yes, there is one.

Annette: Could you creep through the chink so that you can be with them?

(This felt like the most natural next question. It started Lynne's movement towards the all important integration with the separated emotions.)

Lynne: (This was *really difficult* for her.) It feels as if they will overpower me – perhaps eat me – devour me. I'm not big enough to keep them at bay.

(I felt her genuine anxiety here. It reminded me what a huge issue this was for her and how significant the implications might be. It reminded me of the need to keep her safe while moving forward.)

Annette: What are they saying that they want you to hear?

(This was an intuitive leap. I felt that if the emotions might devour her they probably have some issues with her, which they might want to tell her about. The best way to open the channels of communication in relationship problems is always to find out what the other person thinks and feels before telling them about your thoughts and feelings. So, I always encourage clients to listen to the point of view of the feeling-beings or other people in their situation.)

Lynne: "We want peace".

Annette: How could you give this to them?

(An obvious question, which did not move us forward though the answer still gave us valuable information.)

Lynne: I don't know how to.

Annette: Is there anything that you want to say to them?

(Continuing the process of opening up the communication between her and the feeling-beings.)

Lynne: Yes. "Leave me alone!"

(This points to the lack of integration/communication/relationship between Lynne and her feeling-beings.)

Annette: Do they know who you are?

(An intuitive leap towards clarity in the relationship.)

Lynne: No.

Annette: Who are you to them?

(In case this looks like a leading question, I would add that I did not ask this because I thought she might be their mother and was leading her towards this. Her answer came as a great revelation to her and a surprise to me.)

Lynne: Their mother.

Annette: Can you tell them this?

(Continued movement towards integration.)

Lynne: Yes. I really want to give them the peace they ask for but I don't know how. I also want them to go away.

(We're hearing her struggling to choose between nurturing her children and protecting herself from them. Perhaps this is a struggle experienced by her own birth mother? In Chapter Eleven when we asked "What is the difference between labelling and listening to what your intuition is telling you?", I said I would offer some thoughts on this when we explored intuition in detail. This is just such an example of when you might ask whether I have labelled Lynne's response here as mirroring her mother's struggle. All I can say is that the idea not only shimmered through me but rang out that this was a mother walking away from her children or giving them up, which is Lynne's major life issue.)

Annette: Does this mean putting them up for adoption?

(It did feel like an intuitive leap as I asked this question, and her response indicated that it resonated deeply with her.)

Lynne: (She whispered.) I don't know.

Annette: Perhaps you might let them take what they need from you?

(I asked this with great caution and respect for the fear that she had already expressed and then repeats in her next answer.)

Lynne: I'm afraid that they'd eat me.

Annette: What nourishment are they seeking from you by eating you?

(Why would she fear that they would eat her? She had said earlier 'eat or devour me'. This sounds less like an act of aggression than a need for nourishment and I was curious to look at what they want to gain from eating her.)

Lynne: Peace.

(The theme of the feeling-beings wanting peace is running true through this journey.)

Annette: If they are your children and you their mother, perhaps you might want to give them what they need so badly?

(An intuitive leap perhaps, or is this a sort of intuitive logic?[6] But in any case, I was still acutely aware of trying to keep her feeling safe from the fear of being devoured and balancing this with her desire to nurture her 'children' and re-establish her relationship with them.)

Lynne: All right, I'll try. I'll let them come to me.

(This was *extremely courageous* as she was quite frightened here.)

Lynne: I can feel them coming into me through my stomach. This is weird, I can actually feel them, physically inside me, kind of thrashing around. (She

---

6. I make this comment because you may, by now, be becoming so familiar with the intuitive leaps in the questioning that they may no longer appear to you to be making such a quantum leap.

experienced this for a moment or two.) And now they've suddenly turned into a handful of little fishlike things. Now, they're swimming off – inside of me. They seem to be comfortable now, inside me.

What does this mean?

Generally speaking, I do not recommend going into an interpretation of this kind of metaphorical journey with the client. But, as with most of the instructions I have been giving you in this book, there are no absolute rules, just guidelines. In this case, even though Lynne knew that she had arrived at a resolution of her issue, she asked me to give her my sense of what the journey might mean. This is what I said to her.

"It is, of course, far more important for your thoughts about this to be guiding you than for me to offer mine. But since you say that you would really value my giving you my sense of the way your body is connecting with your issues and translating them into metaphor, I will do so. This does not mean to say that I am accurate in this.

"Your abandonment by your parents seems to have been the catalyst for you to have cut off and fragmented from yourself a chunk of your emotions and self associated with this traumatic event. This often happens at the time of a trauma. We cut off a part of ourselves and learn to live without it, but this means that we are not whole. You developed a strong sense of yourself and your femininity throughout your youth, with your (adoptive) mother serving as a strong female role model for a long time. It was only when your marriage failed that these emotions came to the surface and caused your breakdown. One aspect of this was that your strong sense of self and your femaleness was damaged.

"The emotions are fragile and need nurturing, and they suffer when not given attention. You have not been

nurturing this important aspect of yourself, fearing that the emotions are so powerful they would overwhelm you. You have strong issues around safety and so you kept yourself safe by keeping this side of you locked up. The emotions have behaved as children needing love and attention and have become unruly and disruptive. This is a side of you that you have shied away from parenting. The emotions have created symptoms of their anguish by transposing themselves into other areas of your life, motorway driving being one of them.

"The step you took to engage with them and show them that you care for them and love them started a process of loving and accepting this part of yourself. When you feel able to continue to do this, I feel that you will find them/it/you to be little, struggling, unhappy infants rather than an overwhelming tidal wave. When you nurture yourself by loving them/it/you, they will integrate within you and make you whole.

"This is only my sense of this story, so don't be influenced by it. Your thoughts and feelings are far more accurate and you must listen to your inner knowing on this."

The feeling-being

As you read these accounts of conversations between the client and their feeling-beings, some of which you prompt through your intuitive leaps, you may wonder whether it might be appropriate for the coach to talk directly to the feeling-being. In other words, whether you might have a three-way dialogue? My response to this would be a resounding "No". In my view, and this is not shared by some fields of psychology, the coach facilitates the process but is not a part of it. The only reason that the dialogue is useful is because it is the client's inner knowing that is speaking to them – the client's inner wisdom articulating itself through their body at the quantum level. You are not in the client's body and are not party to any of the sensations, whispers and language of their body as they are speaking to them. Your role is to notice the pointers towards the next step of the journey through your client's words, use of metaphor, voice, body language, pauses or hesitation or questions to you. Once you have noticed these, perhaps through the flicker of intuition or a growing awareness based on your observation, you will decide whether to act on them by making an observation or asking a question.

The spotlight is not on the coach at any time; coaching is a totally backstage role in which the coach, the invisible facilitator, merges into the scenery. Your questions to the feeling-being would be irrelevant and might also imply a criticism of the client, almost as if you were talking to their feeling-being about them and mutually suggesting ways that the client might move forward. This would be like discussing an errant child with the parent – in front of the child! Actually, it also feels somewhat schizophrenic to have the feeling-being talking to both the client and you.

Although there is a school of psychology, humanistic psychology, that works in this way, I believe that it is not appropriate for the coach to personally intervene or use themselves as an example within the issue. For example, a female client has a problem in standing her ground with authoritative men, and the coach, a man, asks her how she relates to him as an authoritative male. I believe this would either result in focusing inappropriate or irrelevant attention on the coach or lead to an exploration of the coach/client relationship. Either way, this would impede the process. The only real-life examples I would use in exploring an issue are those of specific people or types of people in the client's life. If the client has an issue with the coach, this is the subject for a different conversation.

So, remembering my session with Tony, you might then ask "If all this is true, why would the coach give the client their personal feedback about their impact upon them?" This is a good question. Now, if this book were a training workshop and someone asked this question, what would the trainer do? The trainer would offer the question back to the group and ask them to discuss it among themselves. In the absence of the rest of the group, I would propose using the question in the same way, to invite you to think about it to deepen your understanding of the quantum skills approach to coaching.

Here, once again, is the feedback that I gave Tony. Might I suggest that you re-read it and then put the book down for a few minutes and think about this question. Try to formulate an answer as to why involving yourself personally with the client is useful in this kind of situation.

I said to Tony:

> *"I know that I'm good at my job, but right now your body language is making me feel uneasy and slightly anxious. If I were working for you, I know I would not be working at my best. You wouldn't be getting the best performance out of me. Now, I want you to know that I'm not telling you this so that you should feel sorry for me. I'm telling you because if I feel this way then it's quite likely that other people do too. And your 360 results seem to indicate that they do."*

* * *

You have probably mulled over a number of possible approaches to this question, and if you feel at ease with the answer you have reached then you are probably right! The answer I would give in the workshop scenario is, by no means, the 'right answer' but is one answer.

If a coach uses their own experience to represent a situation in the client's issue, the focus moves from the client onto the coach. This detracts from the process of the client finding the clues to their issue through their inner knowing. However, when the coach gives feedback about their own experience of the client, the coach is giving a sense of how others experience the client – the essential feedback that we so rarely get an opportunity to hear. It is nothing to do with the coach, actually; it is more of an 'every person's' experience of the client seen through the coach's eyes. And, when the feedback sounds as if the coach is having a negative experience of the client, I would always make the point that I am not giving this feedback to make the client feel guilty or sorry for making me feel this way.

Sometimes, clients will apologise for their impact and this, of course, is totally unnecessary. I would always articulate that I am simply telling them this so that they can get a sense of how others might feel in a similar situation. The coach is still in the background, merely being a mirror through which the client can view their impact. If you have any other thoughts on how to respond in instances such as this I would be delighted to hear them (please email me at Annette@anteri.com.)

CHAPTER SIXTEEN

The power of metaphor and the now

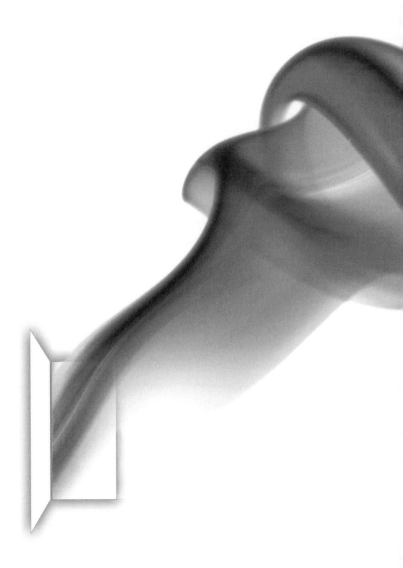

This last case study was a vivid example of a metaphorical journey. A journey moving through the client's issue of fear of motorway driving into the deeper issues that triggered it, using the metaphor created by her inner feelings. In Chapter Nine, we looked at the power of working with metaphor and the idea of metaphorical journeying. Now that we have seen further examples of the use of metaphor in the case studies through the 'feeling-beings', I would like to revisit it and show you another aspect of its potency.

I will summarise and then build upon what we have already covered on the topic of working with metaphor. We talked about how we invite the client to focus on their issue and then to describe the feeling that this generates within the body. When our intuition tells us that there is a disconnected relationship between the client and their inner feelings, we might ask what the feeling itself is feeling about *the client*. The client often sees the feeling as having an identity of its own. We can then start to work with the needs or reactions of this 'feeling-being'.

The quantum tools intuitively lend themselves to working with metaphor as well as personification. As human beings, we readily think about and perceive things in metaphor. Although it is natural for us to perceive a person, thing or event as something else with similar features and talk about it as if it were that thing or represents it, we often do so less and less as we grow older. Children do this quite spontaneously and playfully so perhaps it is this playful, childlike aspect that discourages us from continuing it into adulthood, where we are expected to put our childish ways behind us.

The reason for it being such a useful way of approaching an issue in coaching is that the client doesn't feel that they are talking directly about themselves. *Why is this useful?*

Often, when we talk about something that gives us emotional pain, just hearing ourselves uttering the words that describe it can create quite powerful and sometimes overwhelming emotions. These overwhelming emotions are not the same thing as the emotional pain that we are talking about: it is like another layer of emotion on top of the original one. When this happens, this double layer of emotion may push too many buttons at once and can feel unbearable. All this may make it feel unsafe to talk about the issue any more and cause us to withdraw from the conversation. I am not saying here that the coach should try to prevent the client from crying in a session. Tears, when they occur, are often helpful in breaking down the defensive barriers that may get in the way of an exploration. It is when this 'meta-emotion' (an emotion about an emotion) is in play that a cartload of 'poor me' thoughts may come welling up and diminish the client's ability to work with emotional pain.

The power of the present moment

Why does the meta-emotion diminish the client's ability in this way? It has to do with the power of focusing questions to enable someone to look at a past situation from the vantage point of the present moment. Revisiting the painful situation without the present-centred detachment provided by the focusing questions takes the client back into the past where the event took place and recreates the pain, trauma or embarrassment right there, in the client's body. When you ask the client to remember the painful scenario and, as soon as they arrive there, you ask where in the body they feel it, how big it is, what colour and so on – the client becomes the observer of their pain instead of the victim of it. This transports the client immediately out of the painful past and back into the safety of the present moment. It is as if Scottie has beamed the client up into the safety of the SS Enterprise!

So, when the client can talk about something (such as the feeling-being) that *represents* the elements of the issue, they can talk about the way *it* sees something or what *it* feels or needs in an indirect, less personal way, making the issue easier to explore. Listening to the client's own body-mind talking *through* the feeling-being as if it were another person arouses the client's fascination and interest. "Wow, so this is what's going on here – I never knew that!" This sense of interest, like that of an impartial but concerned observer, is essential for healing, essential for moving through a troublesome issue.

Another essential ingredient for healing is being in the present moment.

The use of metaphor takes the client into their body and into the present moment. As part of my training as a coach, I had to write a thesis on a topic of my choosing to do with the coach's role. My first choice of topic was the coach's role in keeping the client in the present moment. At the time, although I instinctively believed this to be key to the coach's role, I had very limited coaching experience and even less experience of working with metaphor, which considerably restricted the scope for exploring this topic. Therefore, I felt that I did not have a sufficiently weighty argument to support this view and chose a different topic.

Over the past years my exploration and experimentation with the material that has become the subject of this book has opened up a fuller appreciation of the truth of this original title for my thesis. Eckhart Tolle's inspired books *The Power of Now*, *Stillness Speaks* and *A New Earth* as well as his brilliant recorded material have been the main source of this increased appreciation of the power of the present moment to transform our lives. I would strongly recommend that you read and listen to his writings and CDs. A participant on a workshop once asked me how I thought that quantum skills for coaches would develop. My answer was that I have no clear idea, it will go where it will, but I do feel it will increasingly embrace Tolle's teachings as it journeys there.

CHAPTER SEVENTEEN

Power and confidence

Part of the human condition in this brief period that we call
our lifetime is the relentless search for identity and purpose.
As we struggle to find ourselves in the events, relationships
and successes in our life, how vulnerable we are to the ebb
and flow of our level of our personal power. Sometimes we
feel so full of confidence that nothing can touch us and then
in a flash something or someone comes along and reduces it
to dust. In your coaching practice, you have no doubt
discovered that this is an affliction that touches many people,
even some who, on the surface at least, seem to be brimming
with confidence, self-esteem, personal power, a strong sense
of self. Call it what you will.

Caroline Myss, in *Anatomy of the Spirit* makes a strong case
for personal power being necessary for health. She says:

> *"Power is at the root of the human experience. Our
> attitudes and belief patterns, whether positive or negative,
> are all extensions of how we define, use or do not use
> power. Not one of us is free from power issues."*

As a coach, your overall role is to enable clients to become
the finest version of themselves that they can possibly be: to
unlock and reinhabit all the rooms of their castle, to step fully
into themselves and recognise the true greatness there.

Because it sounds like dominance over others, power is one
of those 'hot' words (like 'control' or 'ego') that can trigger
negative buttons in others unless you first define what you
mean by them. In talking about power I mean personal power,
internal power. I am not talking about any of the external
sources of power such as the hierarchal power of your
position or role in an organisation; financial power; the
physical power you may have as a result of your size or
strength; political power; or the power you gain from being
the most skilled or the most knowledgeable in your field. All
of these forms of power, which are bestowed on us from
outside, can also be taken away either by another person's
decision or by their superseding us.

The power that emanates from within us, commonly called self-confidence or self-esteem, is not given to us nor can it be taken away. It is generated from within and when we are in our full personal power we are healthy and we feel strong, confident and calm. We know our own worth and do not need to flaunt it, defend ourselves, compete with others, exert our power over them or gain more power by taking someone else's. In fact, we celebrate when those around us are also in their power.

When people talk about self-confidence, self-esteem or personal power, they often talk about 'not having enough of it' as if it were a thing that you *have* that might come in measures like a handful, a bucketful or even a cartload if you are lucky. They may say things like "If I had more self-confidence, I'd train for the job I'd really like to do and then I'd be more fulfilled" or "If I had more self-esteem, I wouldn't let my boss speak to me like that and I'd be happy." As they say such things, they are putting the future state of *being* on hold as they await the blessed day when they *have* enough of this stuff called confidence to do the thing they want to do that will lead them to being happy, safe and more fulfilled.

This is back-to-front thinking. Self-esteem or personal power is not a thing we have, it is a way of *being*. It is our birthright, our default setting – like happiness. When I talk about 'being in your power' it is exactly this. Your being is rooted in the life source, which is unlimited power to do and have whatever you desire. It is the state of 'being' (powerful/happy/fulfilled/safe) that enables the having and doing, and not the other way around. This is another crucial belief for the coach to hold and live by, for, when this becomes an integral part of your own experience, you will automatically have the insights to reveal to the client the source of their own power and enable them to step into it.

However, just like the photon in the experiment, whatever you perceive it to be, it will appear to be. If the client believes that personal power is a commodity that comes in sprinklings or a bucketful which can run out or be taken away, it will surely behave as if it is. The client will experience it to be true, and the client will be right. Quantum theory says so. In fact, when talking about something "diminishing my confidence", the client can even identify the specific people and events that are able to perform this appalling act time and time again. But, however real this may feel, it is of course not true! When we feel that someone or something has robbed us of our power, we have simply given it away.

And why on earth would we do that? The most eloquent answer to this that I have ever read is that offered by Marianne Williamson in *Return to Love* and which Nelson Mandela chose to include in his inaugural speech:

> *"Our deepest fear is not that we are inadequate. Our deepest fear is that we are powerful beyond measure. It is our light, not our darkness, that most frightens us. We ask ourselves, who am I to be brilliant, gorgeous, talented and fabulous? Actually, who are you not to be? You are a child of god. Your playing small doesn't serve the world. There's nothing enlightened about shrinking so that other people won't feel insecure around you. We were born to make and manifest the glory of god that is within us. It's not just in some of us; it's in everyone. And as we let our own light shine, we unconsciously give other people permission to do the same. As we are liberated from our own fear, our presence automatically liberates others."*

That is the 'why' of the question "Why on earth would we do that?". It can just be too scary to step into our full and glorious self. And just how do we do this bad thing to ourselves? Well, we have a whole variety of self-sabotaging methods.

How we give away our power

Let's return to Caroline Myss' observation:

"Our attitudes and belief patterns, whether positive or negative, are all extensions of how we define, use or do not use power."

Our attitudes and belief patterns, as we have seen throughout this book, produce our behaviour. In other words, it is very obvious to others, from just watching us in action, the exact extent to which we own or disown our power, stand in its light or give it away. What's more, we are all experts on assessing in others, just by seeing their behaviour, the degree to which they are standing in their power or giving it away (although mostly subconsciously). We do not think to ourselves "Hmmm . . . This chap is giving his power away to me. Shall I take it, I wonder?" But, if we also believe that power is a commodity or we secretly despise them for presenting themselves in that way, we might just do it. "Hey, it's on offer, why not!", particularly if we are feeling somewhat powerless ourselves.

And what is it in the person's behaviour that gives away this treacherous information?

The list is endless but here are some factors:

in the face

- Lack of eye contact
- Infrequent smiling
- Quality of the smile – fleeting, nervous, worried
- General composure of facial muscles and facial expressions.

other body language of every description

- Drooping or sagging posture
- Twitching or fiddling with hands

- Hesitant walk
- Awkward ungraceful movement
- General lack of coordination.

voice and speech

- Jerky breathing
- Rapid, nervous speech
- Inappropriate laughter
- Waffling or muddled communication.

Invisible factors such as negative self-talk also contribute. For example, when someone says to themselves "Why are you so stupid", "People think you look ridiculous."

Mannerisms such as these may be marked or quite subtle but they will still carry forth the message "I feel less than you." The ultimate carrier of the bad tidings, though, is the quantum soup. Everything is connected to everything else and (guess what) everything is energy! So, if someone feels less than another person or less than others in general, the energy of this depleted power will transmit itself straight to those others.

Most people do not consciously take others' power away but they might do so if it is given to them on a plate. This is, perhaps, because generally speaking people are so concerned with themselves, their life and how they feel at any one time that they do not pay nearly as much attention to others as one might think. So, when they meet someone who is giving their power away, they do not think about it very much. They tend to react unconsciously towards somebody in the same way that the person invites them to. If, through their body language, the person is silently saying "I'm not as good as you", they will treat them as such. This serves only to reinforce the disabling belief, and the vicious cycle continues.

Therefore, in coaching clients into stepping into their power, i.e. confidence coaching, we need to enable them to show themselves to others in the way that will elicit confidence-affirming responses from others.

As we have already established, many people feel a lack of self-esteem, so I am never surprised to find that a client expresses a need, either by asking directly or through their behaviour, for some coaching in this area of confidence building. The following case study, although a real example, is very typical of the kind of process that I might lead such a client through.

Case Study Six

Philip is a middle manager in his early forties, quiet, unassuming, competent and a good communicator. He said that the main issue he wanted to work on was his lack of self-esteem and I asked him what he meant by this.

> Philip: It's a lack of confidence in my life generally – work and private life. It's difficult to strike up personal relationships. I'm afraid of failing and also of being rejected. I've been divorced twice and this has knocked my confidence a lot.
>
> Annette: What would being confident look like to you?
>
> Philip: Hmm . . . Lots of things. I'd like to be able to think that I could strike up a conversation with a total stranger for example.
>
> Annette: How would you feel physically if you were in a café and contemplating striking up a conversation with a stranger?
>
> Philip: I'd feel frightened and my stomach would be turning over.
>
> Annette: Ok. So can you remember any time in your life when you felt fully confident, as confident as you'd like to be now?
>
> Philip: (He had difficulty in remembering such a time and thought about it for quite a long time.) Well, I was pretty successful in sports at school.

Annette: Which sports were you good at?

Philip: Rugby, football, athletics and basketball. It was good. It gave me a lot of credibility with others – boys and girls. And it gave me immense confidence.

Annette: Wow, this is quite an outstanding achievement. It's pretty amazing that it took you so long to remember something as major as this. Something that gave you immense confidence.

Philip: Yes, but it was a long time ago.

Annette: You know, Philip, the fact that you have experienced such tremendous levels of confidence in your life is an indicator that you absolutely have the potential to tap straight back into it. We can work on this together. So, I'm going to ask you to go back to this time, at school, when you used to feel this amazing confidence. Remember it and feel the way you felt at the time. How does it feel in your body?

Philip: It's a good feeling inside – like I'm smiling inside and standing tall. It's as if I'm up on my toes – feeling 'up for it' with lots of 'get up and go'. I feel a lot of satisfaction in what I'm achieving. Actually I feel bullet-proof, as if nothing can touch me.

Annette: If, feeling like this, you were an animal what animal would you be?

Philip: A lion.

Annette: How would you feel now if you were in the café and contemplating talking to a stranger? A woman.

Philip: It would be easy. I'd just smile and ask her something.

Annette: How do you think she might feel?

Philip: Pretty comfortable. Relaxed. Interested perhaps.

Annette: How would you expect her to respond?

Philip: She'd probably smile back and answer me.

Annette: How would that make you feel?

Philip: Good. I'd feel relaxed and confident too.

Annette: Are you feeling that now?

Philip: Yes. It feels great.

Annette: So, this is your 'lion energy'. How easy was it to step into it just now when I asked you to?

Philip: Easy. Really easy. I can just remember how it feels and it's there.

Annette: And you can do the same thing in exactly the same way whenever you choose. Register how this feels in your body and choose to step into it. If you try it often in easy-to-handle situations, it'll become a familiar process for you, and more and more you will find yourself able to step into it when the situation is more challenging.

(I showed him the kinesiology exercise described in Chapter Nine to reinforce the ease with which we can choose one state of mind over another.)

Using the metaphor of an animal is a useful way to identify the quality of the energy that the client wishes to connect with, and I use this idea in a variety of such situations. Here I started by asking Philip to remember a time when he felt as confident as he would like to feel, to register how this feels within his body and then to work with the animal metaphor to name the energy so that he can reconnect with it at will.

There is no fixed way of working with a tool such as the animal metaphor. So here is another example to show you how to use it in a slightly different way.

Case Study Seven

I had had a couple of sessions with John, a senior manager who wanted to work with me on his communication skills. He had told me that he was not as confident in his interactions with others as he would like, which was due to his low self-image. Like Philip, John was divorced and he felt that this exacerbated the issue.

In the early sessions, I introduced John to the idea of the awareness muscle, basic quantum theory, how energy works and affirmations. This is an extract from his third or fourth session.

> John: I haven't done the affirmations yet – it feels difficult to blow my own trumpet and tell everyone how good I am.
>
> Annette: Ok. So how would you describe your positive qualities?
>
> John: Well, I think I'm a good listener but I'm not good at talking.
>
> Annette: Good. What else?
>
> John: I support my staff well, particularly my deputy.
>
> Annette: That's good. What are your other qualities?
>
> John: I can't think of any others.
>
> Annette: Can you think of someone you admire?
>
> John: Yes I can. He's a friend of mine. He is all the things I'm not.
>
> Annette: What are his qualities?
>
> John: He's very outgoing in a way that brings out the best in me. It makes me able to open up. He's quite bubbly, sort of effervescent, and when I talk to him it makes me feel less reserved and inhibited. He draws me out – almost as if, being the opposite pole to me, he makes me behave more like him.
>
> Annette: How do you feel when you are being drawn out like this and behaving in this less inhibited way?
>
> John: It feels good but it's not me.
>
> Annette: How do you think other people around you feel when you are in this mode?
>
> John: I think it's easier for the extroverts to be around me when I'm like this. They probably find it less effort to talk to me.
>
> Annette: What do you see that makes you think this?
>
> John: Well, I do notice that they seem to respond to me more positively.
>
> Annette: How does this change things in the interaction?
>
> John: It feels like it creates a kind of positive spiral. And this produces a knock-on effect that makes me feel better too.

Annette: You've talked about the effect on the extroverts. How do the introverts respond when you're in this mode?

John: They generally seem to feel more comfortable and responsive as well. It seems to make them feel more able to contribute themselves. I feel as if I'm more approachable to others generally.

Annette: So, from what you say and what you observe it looks as if when you're in this mode it benefits not only you but other people too – both introverts and extroverts.

John: Yes, I think it does.

Annette: You know something? Two things actually! The only reason you can see these qualities in him – being outgoing, bubbly, bringing out the best in others – is because you have these qualities yourself. We only see in others those qualities (and faults) that we see in ourselves. The second thing proves the first one and it's this. The fact that you can be like this when you are with someone like this shows that it *is how you are* – otherwise you couldn't just step into this mode so easily.

(We talked about this idea for a while.)

Annette: So, if you were an animal when in this outgoing mode, what animal would you be?

John: A dog. Though actually I don't like dogs very much!

Annette: That's fine. It doesn't matter at all. What are the qualities of a dog that you recognise in yourself when you're in this mode?

John: Hmm . . . Well he's 'man's best friend' and he bonds and gives comfort. His energy feeds off yours; it's a two-way exchange of energy.

Annette: When you're in 'dog mode', what would others see differently about you?

John: They'd probably see me taking the lead more instead of just sitting back and letting others initiate things.

Annette: What kinds of things?

John: Things like offering suggestions as to things to do, telling them about my experiences and telling anecdotes. And looking more positive.

Annette: What do you mean by 'looking more positive'?

John: A few years ago, I attended a junior management course in which I was videoed giving a presentation. I got the feedback that I appeared confident because I leant forwards in my seat towards the audience. I didn't take this onboard because I don't believe I am confident. Now, though, I can see that I am really a confident person who behaves as if he's not. (When he said this, my heart leapt with joy.) I think, with little effort, I can present myself with confidence in the right circumstances, looking attentive and more confident about contributing.

Annette: Tell me more about being 'confident about contributing'.

John: I have a fear about contributing.

Annette: What are you fearful of?

John: Well, now I try to think of something, I can't think of anything really.

Annette: So, what could go wrong if you contributed more?

John: Nothing, apart from looking a fool. But this is probably a fear that most people have, isn't it? But it hardly ever materialises.

Annette: Yes, it is. You'd be surprised how common it is. So, do you think a dog is fearful of looking a fool?

John: No, he's not. That's right! What happens when I move into 'dog mode' is that I find that, for whatever reason, mainly because the extravert in the group has drawn me out enough, I can suddenly switch into contributing with confidence in all kinds of situations.

Annette: You say this happens 'for whatever reason'. It seems to me that this is the key. Right now, you are dependent upon someone else to flick this switch to put you in 'dog mode', and it's great when it happens but you have no control over it.

John: Yes, that's exactly it!

Annette: You know we have a measure of choice and control over what we are aware of. What we are unaware of controls us.[7] So let's see if we can work at helping you to gain awareness of this mode and find the switch so that you can flick it on yourself.

John: Ok. Great!

Annette: Right then. So, see if you can remember a time when you were in dog mode, confidently chatting in an outgoing way, telling anecdotes and stories and things. (He did this.) Now see if you can intensify this experience. Try turning up the volume. What are you feeling in your body as you do this?

John: My shoulders and throat feel tingly and it's leaking downwards into my upper arms too. My face feels a little tight from the unfamiliarity of smiling a lot.

Annette: This is great! Now come out of this mode.

John: Ok, I'm out of it now.

Annette: And, now go back into it again.

John: Ok. I'm back in it again. But, this is interesting. I didn't go back into it as I did the first time, through the memory of the experience. I just decided to recreate the physical sensations in my shoulders. It's weird. It was enough to put me into 'dog mode'. And it has actually created the feeling of confidence.

(Again, I was so thrilled when he made this discovery independently of any prodding from me.)

Annette: So, John, this is the switch you are looking for! Hey, that was easy! What you've just learned is the skill of adjusting your physiology by putting your awareness on it. *We have a measure of choice and control over what we are aware of.* Therefore, you now have the ability to switch this feeling on inside yourself upon demand. It's a brand new skill and you will need to practise it often to have it to hand right when you need it.

---

7. Whitmore (2002).

John: Yes. This is amazing. And it's easy. I really think I can use this in all kinds of scenarios.
(We discussed a few of the possible scenarios. The biggest barrier seemed to be that of meeting new women, so we explored this a little further.)

Annette: How do you feel your voice sounds when you're in 'dog mode'?

John: It's different. Probably softer, more rounded, less hard-edged, a bit more open and vulnerable like when I'm laughing. But there are dangers in being open.

Annette: What are the dangers?

John: Failure, rejection, losing credibility.

Annette: How often do these dangers materialise?

John: Not often.

Annette: When you are open, in 'dog mode', where is the spotlight?

John: It's on other people but not on me.

Annette: Where is your attention?

John: Away from me, too.

Annette: And where is your attention when you're in inhibited mode?

John: It's on myself.

Annette: So, then, this is a second switch! You've just said that, to be in 'dog mode', you have to take your attention off yourself and direct the beam towards others. So, now imagine it as a spotlight in your solar plexus and just swivel it around to shine outwards towards others.

John: Yes, I can feel this! This is the secret that no one told me!

Annette: Yes, it is. When you forget about yourself – how you appear to others, what they might be thinking about you, how you might compare yourself to them – and become truly interested in the people around you, self-confidence flows in buckets, especially if you're using your 'first switch' at the same time! And doing this is genuine for you, as you are naturally a good listener anyway.

I spoke to John recently. He is still single but a lot more confident and at ease with himself.

Analysis of Case Study Six and Case Study Seven

You can see from these case studies examples of the different ways in which we can use the animal metaphor in confidence coaching. This is to demonstrate that there is no set formula for working with a metaphor like this but the central elements for their use are similar, as follows:

We are connecting to the client's past experience of a time when he felt confident

This is the main element of John's case study. The energy of this memory still resonates within his body, and his body-mind is able to work with it even though his conscious mind might block this inner knowing. As John said, "I can see that I am really a confident person who behaves as if he's not." At a conscious level, he believes and feels that he is not confident, so he would probably be unable to work directly with this memory as it contradicts his core belief about himself. So, we step into the safe, indirect world of metaphor where he can playfully describe the qualities of the confidence through the persona of an animal. The final step is then to develop the skill of 'stepping into' the animal and enabling the body-mind to own the qualities of confidence that it remembers.

Once Philip had reconnected with the experience of confidence, I asked him to identify the qualities of this confidence and we then linked it to the animal that possesses these qualities for him. John also recalled a particular situation in which he felt confident but this time I asked him to identify the animal that represented the energy of this confidence, and from this he was able to describe the qualities of that animal.

The client knows that he is describing himself and this knowing resonates in his energy system

A second element that these two approaches have in common is that, as the client describes the qualities of the animal, he knows that he is describing himself and this knowing resonates in his energy system. But, because it is 'only an animal', he is not tempted to slip into his usual self-deprecating thinking patterns and discount it by saying "But I'm not like this." So the work is done at a quantum level, energetically, before his conscious mind has time to intervene and say "This is silly."

The coach uses these revelations

The third element is that, as the client reveals his memories of confidence and the qualities of the chosen animal, the coach uses these revelations to encourage him to see that this is his true, powerful self. This encouragement is a vital part of the client's connection to his power. When Philip told me about his experience of immense confidence in the sporting arena, I assured him that "The fact that you have experienced such tremendous levels of confidence in your life is an indicator that you absolutely have the potential to tap straight back into it." I told John that the only reason he could see the qualities he admired in his friend was because he has these qualities himself. I believe both of these statements to be absolutely true. For statements of encouragement like these to resonate with the client's inner knowing about his true power and increase his growing sense of self-esteem, they have to be genuine. This means the coach has to believe these statements. So here are two more keystone beliefs a coach must hold.

Keystone beliefs a coach must hold

Let's just pause for a moment and sum up the keystone beliefs that we have identified so far.

1. See the client as whole, healthy and good and accept them for who they are without judgement

I described why this is vital in Chapter Fourteen.

2. Good health and happiness are our 'default settings' as human beings

This is also covered in Chapter Fourteen.

3. If we have experienced a deep sense of power and confidence at any time in the past, we can step back into it

The reason that this is true, is of course, to do with the quantum nature of this successful event. The resonance of the energy of this power-generating event in our life is still within us and able to be fired up again at the flick of a switch. The trick is to find the switch. You will have experienced this in your own life; try to recall it.

My first memory of this was when I was seventeen and in a competition sponsored by an international volunteer service organisation to be chosen for a six-week trip to the United States. The final stage in the selection process was to give a ten-minute talk to the selection committee, which, at seventeen, felt utterly terrifying. And I won! I felt great, and experienced a great surge of confidence that I had never felt before. A few years later in a job interview where I wanted to feel this kind of confidence again, I wore the same jacket that I wore on the evening of the terrifying talk and got the job. Through wearing that jacket, I learnt to operate my power switch. It was nothing to do with the jacket of course, but it was a symbol.

Using symbols in this way is a premise of neuro linguistic programming (NLP), which you may be familiar with. You saw in the session with John how we identified two confidence-enabling switches from his own experience.

4. We only recognise qualities in others that we have ourselves

To recognise a quality is to value it, and the reason we value it is that it is within us – it is a part of our value system. We may not recognise or realise this, though, and may therefore not demonstrate these qualities in our actions. This can lead us to believe that someone else may have these qualities but we do not. The coach's job is to show the client who believes this, as John did, that the quality is there but that for some reason he is not allowing it to shine through. The reason is often one of the following:

- A fear of failure of letting it shine
- A feeling of being less than someone he admires who clearly has this quality
- A fear of looking stupid.

Holding these keystone beliefs and being able to recount them to the client at moments when it would reassure or encourage them, is a gift that you offer. Why? Because as the coach you have, whether or not you recognise it, a certain degree of authority. You know about these things. You are the 'expert' in all this stuff, aren't you? And, if you assert that this is how things are, in the same matter-of-fact way that you might talk about the laws of gravity, the client will believe you. You know that, if the client believes these things, the client will apply them and achieve the confidence (or whatever the client is aiming for) that they desire. So, use this influence to your advantage in the service of the client's goals. Clients have frequently told me that the fact that I believed a particular idea with such certainty gave them the confidence to believe it, too, and enabled them to put it into action in their lives. This is the gift you offer your client.

When the client cannot recall past confidence

Sometimes, however, the client cannot recall feeling confident. This may produce a sadness as the client realises this, and maybe in you too. I would urge you here not to react to this, even internally. Do not show that you feel sorry for the client and say (or even think), "Oh, that's sad. I'm so sorry." This will create a secondary emotion of "Yes, it is sad. My life is sad. Poor me", which will derail the coaching process as you attempt to console your client. Knowing that you have such familiarity with people's life experiences, the fact that you are surprised by your client's will make them feel unusual, abnormal even, which may be worrying to them.

Although it is sad, it is not uncommon that someone cannot remember feeling confident in the past. Like anything else that the client says, this should be treated as information that you can work with. The coach should be unshockable but empathic and calm. Your sympathetic but understanding and reassuring facial expression and body language will enable the client to accept this realisation calmly as if it is nothing out of the ordinary. My approach to working with this is then to ask the client to think of someone they admire, someone who seems to be confident in the way the client would like to be. (Note that I don't say "seems to have the confidence you would like to have". I always try to steer clients away from the idea of confidence being something 'to have' rather than 'to be'.)

You may remember that John had difficulty in naming his qualities but continually mentioned his shortcomings. I did not focus on these at all, but moved forward in the way I have just described until we found a strength to work with. Here it is again:

> Annette: How would you describe your positive qualities?
> John: Well, I think I'm a good listener but I'm not good at talking.
> **(He names a quality but adds a failing.)**

Annette: Good. What else?

John: I support my staff well, particularly my deputy.

(I could have built on this by asking how he supports his deputy. This would have taken us down a different pathway that may have been equally useful.)

Annette: That's good. What are your other qualities?

John: I can't think of any others.

(He looked a little crestfallen here.)

Annette: Can you think of someone you admire?

John: Yes I can. He's a friend of mine. He is all the things I'm not.

(Back to self-criticism.)

Annette: What are his qualities?

John: He's very outgoing in a way that brings out the best in me. It makes me able to open up. He's quite bubbly, sort of effervescent, and when I talk to him it makes me feel less reserved and inhibited. He draws me out – almost as if, being the opposite pole to me, he makes me behave more like him.

(Talking about someone who has the qualities John admires made him more animated, enthusiastic and verbal. This is a key moment in the session where he relates his experience of being more outgoing and confident and this gives us something dynamic to work with.)

Annette: How do you feel when you are being drawn out like this and behaving in this less inhibited way?

(I try to help him register the feeling in his awareness muscle. And, of course, I use his words, "less inhibited".)

John: It feels good but it's not me.

(His perception of his own lack of qualities is always at the forefront of his mind and he will make a reference to them at every opportunity.)

Annette: How do you think other people around you feel when you are in this mode?

(I do not get drawn into his feeling of 'less than' but build on the outcomes of his feelings of confidence. Though, because he has not used this word to describe this 'mode of being', I

> **do not use it either. Now that he is engaged in the interesting**
> **process of exploring the effects of confident behaviour, he**
> **stops reverting back to telling me about his weaknesses.)**

This process of asking the client to recall a time he felt confident or working with the qualities of someone he admires can be used in whatever context you need. It might be confidence building or behaving more assertively, more playfully, more gently and so on.

As you use this approach with or without using the animal metaphor, you are, in effect, working with the visualisation process. The client is visualising the mode they are trying to embed in their behavioural and thinking patterns through the energy of the animal, the words they use or both.

Sometimes a client may feel that connecting with an animal does not work. Not everyone will relate to it. If not, that's fine too. Just work with whatever the client brings up.

CHAPTER EIGHTEEN

Problem solving and creative thinking

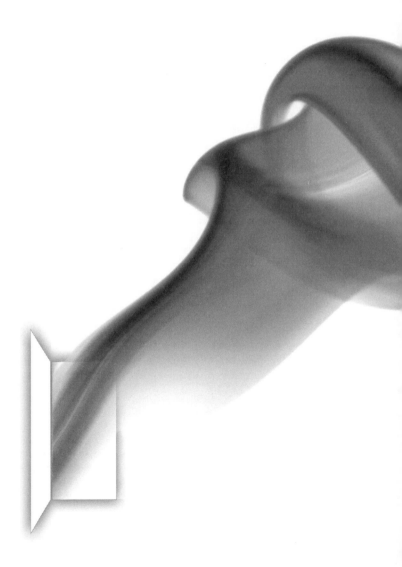

In Chapter Nine, I described the analogy of the human brain being like a pile of sand. I talked of the need, when solving a problem, to create a pile of sand (or mindset) that would be different from the one we had when we created the problem.

Many of the quantum tools we have been looking at can help the client to do just that, to create a new pile of sand to look at the problem in a different way. Coaching should do more than help clients to see problems in different ways: it should give them the skills to approach all their problems like this so that they are not dependent upon the coach to obtain a different view of problem situations. Therefore, I often teach my clients creative thinking tools as part of the tool kit. To teach clients may not sound like pure coaching, and we discussed in Chapter One why these quantum skills seem to break the rules of coaching in this way. To teach clients to think creatively and freely is teaching them to fish rather than merely giving them a gift of fish.

Appreciative enquiry[8] is a simple and dynamic tool for creating new piles of sand. I share this tool with clients and would encourage you to do so too. If you find that the way I explain it here resonates with you, you might choose to present it to your clients in a similar way.

The problem-solving mindset

The Chinese word for 'crisis' is composed of two pictograms, the first of which means 'danger'. It is this aspect of a crisis that first strikes us as we face a problem situation that we need to resolve. The threat presented by the issue is right there before us, staring us in the face – intimidating, looming and undermining our wellbeing. We do not want it there and we resist it. Something has gone terribly wrong. This was not

---

8. Originally called 'Appreciative Inquiry' and conceived in 1987 by Dr David Cooperrider and colleagues at Cape Western Reserves School of Organizational Behaviour.

part of the plan we had for ourselves. We need to move towards what we want and away from this alarming situation. So we turn our back on the problem and seek the solution elsewhere.

But remember, there are two pictograms. The second one is that of 'opportunity', the other side of the coin to the aspect of danger – the other half of the story of the problem. When we turn our back on the problem in search of the solution, we also turn our back on the opportunity that it offers.

If we relate this to the ancient Chinese wisdom of the yin yang symbol, we see that the seed of the solution is found within the problem situation itself, not outside it.

How do we access the solution? We need to return to the acceptance of the present moment. As long as we label the problem as 'bad' and the solution as 'good', we are polarising these two aspects of the situation, two aspects that are simply opposite sides of the same coin. They are the same thing seen from different angles. So the first step is to know that this is true.

The next step is to consciously accept the situation. This does not mean you have to persuade yourself to be happy about it. Obviously, you cannot be happy about something that throws up a great big challenge to you. But you can accept it and be peaceful about it rather than let it throw you into turmoil. Eckhart Tolle talks about "not resisting what is", that is to say, not saying "No" to what is. When you internally say "No, I don't want this", your body responds similarly and you are in effect saying "No" with your whole energy system. At a quantum level, this energy of resistance is fighting against, rather than engaging with, the energy of the problem event, and the opportunity will thus remain embedded in it and unavailable to you. So say "Yes" to the situation. "Yes, I accept that this is how it is", not "Yes, I am happy about it." This links back to the giving-up-being-irritated exercise in Chapter Eight.

Once you have accepted the problem situation, you can get curious about it. You know the opportunity is in there somewhere; you just have to find it. Asking "I wonder where it is?" will help. Curiosity is the key, and the appreciative enquiry tool offers some great curiosity-filled questions to ask yourself.

Appreciative enquiry

A few years ago, on an icy Saturday morning in January, my husband and I had a busy day ahead of us; shopping and a stack of other tasks had to be done. The following afternoon, we were due to leave for a three-hour drive for an overnight stay in a hotel ready for a training course we were running together on the Monday. My husband got up early and went to play tennis with friends and then, at 10.30 or so, we hopped in the car to go shopping. It would not start. You can imagine the kind of instant reaction this produced in us. "Of all the days for this to happen – just when we have so much to do", garnished with one or two inevitable expletives! The battery was flat and we had to call our neighbour for a jump start so that we could go and buy a new one. Our car, being a slightly unusual model, needed a hard-to-find kind of battery and we felt frustrated at the pressure to get it fitted before our trip the following day.

In the midst of all this, I decided to step into 'Pollyanna mode' and asked "Ok, so what's good about this, then?" and we put our resistance to the situation aside while we tried to find some things that were good about it. We came up with a few ideas:

- It is a three-year old car, the battery is probably getting a bit tired, so it was bound to go sometime soon

- At least Terry was able to get out to play tennis before it died
- If it had gone later in the day, we would not have had enough time to find the correct battery
- If it had gone on Sunday afternoon, we would not have been able to make the journey to the training venue and it would have been too late to hire a car.

And we realised that, in fact, this was the perfect time for it to go. It left us the time we needed to fit the new battery and, by speeding up a little, we managed to complete all the other things on our list too. So, all in all, we felt that we were being looked after and the whole situation looked much more cheery. Nothing had changed, and it was not as if we even had to find a solution to a problem, but it did change the whole day for us. Instead of stewing and pouting, we went in search of the battery with some buoyancy without losing the quality of the weekend.

This rather mundane example shows how we can learn to practise saying "Yes" to what is and asking these curiosity-filled questions about the everyday glitches that crop up in our lives. Questions like:

- What's good about this?
- How can I use this situation?
- What else could this mean?
- How does this serve me?
- What can I learn here?
- What am I assuming here?
- What am I assuming that makes me see this as a problem?
- What information do I not have that, if I did have, might help me to see this situation differently, and how can I get it?
- What else might it mean?

■ What's the worst thing that could happen?
  – What would happen if I allowed this to take place?
  – And then what would happen?
  – And what might that mean?
  – What would be good about that?

Just asking questions like these will start to make you feel more upbeat and interested in the problem and create the new pile of sand. Then the answers you find will continue to reflect this upward spiralling energy and take you to a constructive, proactive place, freeing you from the tyranny of the predicament. These are also great questions to ask a team that feels stuck in a problem.

You might decide to find ten good answers to such a question and keep on searching until you do so. These are actually very powerful coaching questions, so in successfully teaching your clients to use them, you are teaching them self-coaching skills.

Brainstorming

Brainstorming is the best-known creative thinking tool and is widely used in organisations across the globe. It can be conducted either as a group activity or as a personal problem-solving tool. The basic rules in either context are:

■ No idea should be discounted or regarded as too silly
■ Every idea should be noted down.

It is a valuable tool for coaches, as they encourage their clients to think more freely about their issues, as illustrated in the next case study.

Case Study Eight

Jeremy had attended our workshop on coaching skills for managers but was finding it difficult to create 'coaching opportunities' with his staff and was continuing to offer advice as he had in the past. We brainstormed different ways that might make it easier for him to remember to coach his team. This generated several ideas and this is how we explored one of them.

The idea was for Jeremy to keep a chair by his desk so that people would feel invited to sit in it. As they did this, it would remind Jeremy to ask coaching questions rather than offer solutions. This sounded like a good scheme but the issue he foresaw was how to stop other people from moving the chair away from beside his desk. We brainstormed this too, and came up with the following ideas:

- Put a label on the chair
- Tie it to the ground
- Tell people what it is for
- Ask Jeremy's secretary to make sure it stays there
- Get a different coloured chair
- Get a comfy chair
- Put a cushion on it
- Put a teddy or some other 'friendly being' on it.

We discussed these ideas individually and, by the end of the week, Jeremy had gone ahead and ordered a comfy chair that was to be delivered within two weeks. In the intervening period, he used an office chair, which he called 'Jeremy's chair', and to make it more welcoming he put a teddy bear on it. He found that even this interim arrangement worked well and served as a trigger for him to stop what he was doing and give his full attention to the person sitting in the chair. The conversations he had were relaxed and productive and even within a couple of weeks changed the team dynamic considerably.

Reverse brainstorming

A variation on this theme is reverse brainstorming. This means that, instead of generating ideas to solve the problem, you think of ways in which you could make it worse. This does not mean that you actually try to make it worse, but simply that it loosens the idea-generating process even further and enables the truly wacky ideas to surface. Then, one or two of these ideas serve as a springboard for returning to possible ways to solve the problem. Like regular brainstorming, this is a technique that can be used very effectively in groups as well as with an individual.

Andrew was responsible for designing and implementing a new system within his organisation but was being confronted with blockages at every turn, including finding the funding for it. We brainstormed how Andrew could make the situation worse:

- Stop working
- Do not do anything about it
- It will get worse all the time – let it!
- Stop trying to reach an equitable solution
- Go and make mischief – there are some big personalities in the organisation. At meetings, 90% of input is mischief-making anyway.

I asked Andrew what would happen if he chose the second idea and did nothing. He said:

- It would get senior visibility very quickly
- He would quite clearly not achieve the task and this would have knock-on effects across all departments
- The operations department would start screaming because their resources would dry up
- The finance department would start screaming because they would not have the necessary system in place

■ It might be a way of obtaining the funding that he
   needed.

As Andrew described these possible outcomes, he could see
that there was the seed of a brilliant idea in this. Although we
were not talking about actually sabotaging the project, this
provided a way of looking at it differently. It showed him that
what he needed to do was to draw attention to the
importance of this new system and the implications for the
organisation if it was not brought into being. We then
brainstormed new ways in which he could achieve this.

CHAPTER NINETEEN

Psychodrama

In Chapter Two, I described the basics of psychodrama and its use in coaching. Like the use of metaphor, it takes clients out of the perceived reality of their situation so that they can see it in a variety of other possible ways. I do not use formal psychodrama methodologies, just the essence of it. For example, I might ask clients to put themselves in the position of one of the aspects of the issue and get a sense of how the situation looks from this new viewpoint.

As you have already seen from the case studies, task overload or time management is an issue that challenges many people and often crops up in coaching sessions. Here then, is another example of exploring this issue using an approach based on psychodrama.

Case Study Nine

Sarah: I tend not to finish things off; I just let them drift.

Annette: Do you ever finish these tasks?

Sarah: Some of them probably just wither on the vine and disappear. My best solution is to put them in a folder, in a filing cabinet and get them out of sight.

Annette: Imagine for a moment that you are one of the unfinished pieces of work that you have put away in the filing cabinet. How do you think you'd feel?

Sarah: I'd say "I've been overlooked. I need to be addressed. When is she going to get round to looking at me?" I am also aware that there are other bits of paper in the cabinet with me. I'm thinking "Doesn't she care about me? Am I of such low value to her that she's not going to give me her attention?"

Annette: Imagine that you start chatting to the other bits of paper. Then all of you get chatting among yourselves? What are you all saying?

Sarah: We'd be saying "Oh, there are others too. I thought it was just me! What is she up to? We're all in the same boat, then?" Hmm . . . Perhaps we could work together to get her attention?"

Annette: And what kind of plan do you think you might come up with?

Sarah: Well, we might try to create a crisis for her, which might force her to look at us.

Annette: What effect might that have on her?

Sarah: It would make her panic. She might freak out. Perhaps it would be more than she could cope with. And then we'd never get seen to.

Annette: What else could you do, that might help her perhaps?

Sarah: Well, if we decided which ones needed to be done first, we could prioritise ourselves for her. Then she'd feel that she was winning the battle.

Annette: Which ones would have the highest priority?

Sarah: There might be ones that would achieve more for her than just getting the task done. Things that might give her more skills in handling all of us, for example. Things that would kind of move her forward in her life, perhaps. It might make her feel better about herself – more confident, less floundering.

I then introduced her to Stephen Covey's time management tool, which I mentioned in Case Study Three in Chapter Twelve.

You can see that the way we are using psychodrama is very similar to the use of the awareness muscle. Instead of exploring the issue from the viewpoint of the feeling within the client, we are using the viewpoint of something external to the client such as:

- A living being such as an animal or plant
- An inanimate object that is situated in the physical space where the problem usually happens – a chair, a filing cabinet, a lamp
- An element of the problem itself, i.e. the 'bits of paper' in the last case study.

It works in the same way as the awareness muscle approach works in that it enables the client to safely explore the issue in a detached, objective way without attaching any disorientating emotions or self-constructed meaning to it. This may sound cold, as if we are avoiding being subjective, real or connected to the issue. Not at all. Actually, we are being more 'real' by working in this way.

Part of what we have been calling 'the human condition' is our tendency to define ourselves and find our identity in our thoughts. We think this is real. It is not real. In fact, most spiritual teachings refer to it as madness. It is also seriously limiting to us as human beings: it is what makes us think we are a two-bedroomed semi in a bad state of repair rather than the awe-inspiring castle that we really are. So, working with these techniques, which takes us out of our usual (piles of sand) thinking framework that defines us and our response to the world, reveals an unbounded version of reality that is nearer the truth. Because it is our feelings or some inanimate object that is observing the process and not us, we do not identify with their commentary or seek to attach our identity to their thoughts. This creates a space for the truth of the situation to be revealed within the pure light of this unattached observation.

This may sound like coaching is straying into the realms of spirituality. Throughout the book we have found that the quantum skills approach does overlap extensively with a number of spiritual principles, and what we might call 'universal laws'. Does this mean that quantum skills coaching is spiritual coaching? We will answer this question now, in the last chapter.

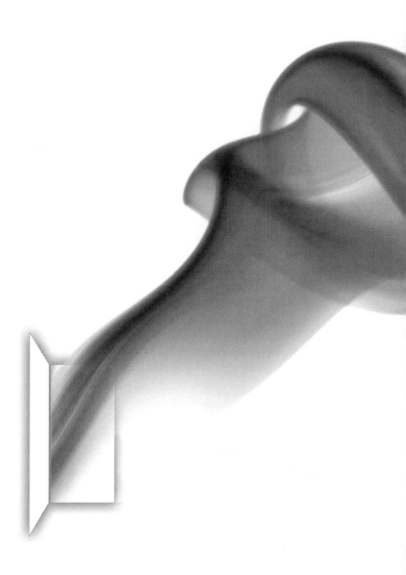

CHAPTER TWENTY

Universal laws

We have already seen that the coach's beliefs will shape their approach to their practice. Quantum skills for coaches has emerged from my beliefs about the quantum nature of the universe, the role of our emotions and the body-mind. These principles are also rooted within many spiritual teachings and the so-called 'universal laws', so it is true that much of the power inherent in this form of coaching is drawn from the spiritual.

I have mentioned universal or natural laws in earlier chapters. What are these laws of the universe? Who decided that they are the laws, and how do we know that they are true?

There is, to my knowledge, no definitive list of universal laws compiled by a certified universal law-maker, but there is great consensus throughout the central spiritual traditions about 'the way things work'. Remember the definition of wisdom I mentioned in an earlier chapter? "Wisdom is understanding the way the world works and working with it to get the results you want."

This is what I mean by universal laws. Because we understand the Law of Gravity, we take care not to run downstairs with trailing shoelaces. Other laws of physics, which have shaped the world we live in and the way we live in it, are the laws of:

- Electromagnetism
- Motion
- Thermodynamics.

They all existed as descriptions of 'the way the world works' long before Newton or Maxwell articulated them as being 'laws of physics'. Thus it is with the spiritual laws or universal laws. Buddhism, Hinduism, Islam, Christianity, A Course in Miracles, to name but a few spiritual teachings, depict the world through these universal laws, and a number of spiritual writers have extracted their interpretations of these laws from these teachings. The movie and the book *The Secret* give a vibrant rendering of the Law of Attraction. Deepak Chopra outlines *The Seven Spiritual Laws of Success* and Dan Millman describes seventeen Laws of Spirit in his book *The Life You Were Born to Live*, to name only a few. And while Eckhart Tolle does not talk about the Law of the Present Moment, his account of the 'power of the now' certainly implies that there is a universal law in play when we practise 'presence'.

I do not get the impression either that these purveyors of universal laws are squabbling among themselves as to which is the 'official version'. Let's just say that the universe operates according to spiritual laws, however we choose to name them, and when we recognise their essence and align our lives with them the results are quite astonishing. Once you experience this, to be living out of alignment with these laws feels like you are pushing the river backwards. Living within them feels like you have flipped over onto your back and are letting the river take you where it will, in its flow. Sometimes you might get tumbled over the rocky places and suffer some bruising, which may manifest as problem situations, relationship issues, emotional pain or ill-health. I talked before about the unfathomable mystery that can present us with life challenges for no apparent reason. But, overall, the power of the river carries you forth into new places of learning, opportunity, adventure and growth.

We will look more closely at these laws. What are they and how do they relate to the quantum skills? Well, in truth, I am not going to describe them all to you but I do recommend that you read the books I have mentioned above as this will unveil all the links I have been referring to. I will, however, outline some of the key connections to universal laws that crop up regularly in the coaching context, in addition to the laws of attraction and intent discussed in earlier chapters.

Law of potentiality

Quantum theory, and the concept of everything being composed of energy, tells part of the story of this spiritual law. If we look very deeply into this law, it takes us well and truly into the spiritual realm so we must be certain to keep the link with this firmly rooted within the context of coaching. As I said very early in this book, the client comes to you for coaching and not for spiritual guidance. If the client recognises that this is spiritual coaching, acknowledge it but do not start spiritual coaching through this unless the client asks specifically for it.

Law of cause and effect, or karma

This natural law is the law of action and its consequences and, in the context of coaching, is described by E+R=O.

(Law of) being in the present

I have mentioned a number of times that I believe a key role for the coach is to help the client to stay in the present moment. Emotions are the most present-centred thing we have in our lives. Therefore the awareness muscle tool, focusing and metaphorical journeying are all techniques for achieving this.

Law of detachment

Have you ever noticed that what you try to grasp eludes you and what you try to get rid of in your life pursues you? This contrary concept often appears when coaching a client who wants and needs recognition or respect from others. The client may behave in ways that seem pushy as they try to get their ideas, intellectual ability, personal worth or contributions acknowledged (and in ways that make sure everyone hears about them). In a coaching session, the client may complain of being overlooked or of having to work overly hard to be recognised (the client means 'noticed' but rarely says this) to little avail, and feels frustrated by expending so much effort. When you work with this, you can point out that the more forcefully the client tries to gain such recognition or attention, the more they are sure of pushing it away. When the client gives up the struggle to gain it and relaxes in the knowledge that they already have it, they are amazed at how effortlessly it comes to them.

This phenomenon invokes the universal laws of attraction, detachment and intention. The visualisation technique in Chapter Four describes in detail how this works. 'Energy flows where attention goes', so when someone tries to grasp or cling onto recognition, they are doing so because they are fearful of not getting it, or of losing it if they do have it. Therefore, the client's attention is on how awful it will be not to have it and that is exactly what the client manifests in life. It is unconscious visualisation, which is almost as powerful as conscious visualisation. Conversely, when a client is trying to get rid of a familiar aspect of their behaviour or life situation, they are often unconsciously fearful of how they will manage without it, even though they believe that they no longer want it. Thus the client's attention is on having it and the energy of this attention causes the situation to linger on.

When coaching clients who are finding that they are not having the impact they would like on others, you will probably find it fruitful to hold this natural law in mind as you explore it with them. Start with the client's self-observation of their behaviour or impact to create a keyhole into the situation, and gently expand this peephole with your questions. You must make it safe for them to do this, and so enable them to let go of the fear that is keeping them from their goal.

Case Study Ten

Peter had been told that his style rubbed people up the wrong way, particularly his team, but he was not sure exactly what it was that he was doing that had this effect.

> Annette: If other people were to describe you as an animal, what animal do you think they might see you as?

Peter: An animal? Hmm . . . Perhaps a dog, an Alsation.

Annette: What do you think it is about an Alsation that they are seeing?

Peter: Gregarious. Outgoing. Confident, I suppose. Quite forthright. Good communicator with original ideas.

Annette: And how does being around this Alsation make them feel?

Peter: Cautious.

Annette: What's the caution about?

Peter: They can see some of his qualities, but they don't give him the credit for them.

Annette: And why does this make them cautious?

Peter: They think he must know his worth because he's so confident, but they don't want to give him the feedback about it. And, actually, now that I look closely at him, I can see that he's wearing a muzzle.

Annette: Who put the muzzle on him?

Peter: They did!

Annette: Why did they do that?

Peter: To keep him down.

Annette: What do they think would happen if he wasn't wearing a muzzle?

Peter: He would bite them – with words.

Annette: What kind of words?

Peter: He wants to tell them that they don't value him enough.

Annette: How would this bite them?

Peter: He feels undervalued – put down. It infuriates him. The words would show this.

Annette: But they see him as an Alsation. You said this is gregarious, outgoing, confident and quite forthright. A good communicator with original ideas. This sounds like they do recognise his value.

Peter: Yes, I think they do. But they don't tell him.

Annette: So he's infuriated because they don't tell him even though they recognise his value?

Peter: Yes.

Annette: What would have to be in place for them to feel
    safe enough to take off the muzzle?

Peter: I suppose they'd have to know that he wouldn't go
    for them. That it was ok for them not to tell him how
    great he was.

Annette: And what would have to happen for them to know
    that?

Peter: He would have to show that he didn't need them to
    tell him all these things.

Annette: And what would have to happen for him not to
    need this?

Peter: He'd have to not need it. Genuinely. He'd have to just
    know that they really did value him.

Annette: Does he know this – really?

Peter: Yes, he does – of course.

Annette: So, is it safe to take off the muzzle now?

Peter: Yes. I can stop trying to get a pat on the head
    whenever I do something good. I know it's appreciated.

Within a couple of weeks of letting go of the need to be
verbally recognised for his contributions, Peter was staggered
to find that his team started to actually give him the feedback
that he previously craved. This scenario is typical of so many
similar situations and is always a source of amazement to the
client.

This aspect of the Law of Attraction is typically present when
coaching a client who is seeking their soul-mate. The more
someone is trying to find their perfect partner while at the
same time fearing that they either do not exist or would reject
them if they did turn up, the more effectively they are building
a partner-proof wall around themselves. The universe, being a
vast copying machine, will manifest either of these self-
fulfilling prophesies in a twinkling of an eye! It has been said
that "the universe corresponds to the nature of your song". If
their song is a desolate song of loneliness and
disappointment, so will be their experience. As you listen to
their song through their words, you will straight away

recognise the harmony of acceptance or the dissonance of resistance.

Develop an attitude of gratitude

I am not sure if this can be called a universal law, but the power inherent in expressing gratitude in our lives certainly has the characteristics of one.

This is something you will have heard countless times and, yes, everything you have heard or read about it is true. Gratitude is the single most important ingredient for a healthy, abundant, love-filled life. To give thanks for everything in your life, whether or not you think it is good, is the key to life. The universe corresponds to the nature of your song, so if your song is one of heartfelt thanks for the gifts you have been given, the universe will give you even more gifts to be thankful for. When 'stuff happens' that you find it hard to be thankful for, the appreciative enquiry approach provides questions to ask yourself that can help to reveal why you can express gratitude for it.

You may remember in Case Study One that I encouraged Michael to focus on the gifts and talents he had been given and to feel a deep gratitude for them. I would warmly encourage you to do the same with your clients, as well as for yourself. It makes a phenomenal difference to our lives and this is, after all, what coaching is about.

Further reading

If you are truly interested in practising quantum skills for coaches I would recommend reading the books marked with an asterisk (*)

Arntz, W., Chasse, B., Vicente, M., 2003: *What the Bleep Do We Know?* (HCI)

What the Bleep Do We Know?, 2004. Film directed by William ARNTZ, Betsy CHASSE and Mark VICENTE. Captured Lights Industries.

Atkinson, M., 2007: *The Mind-Body Bible* (Piatkus)

* Bays, B., 1999: *The Journey* (Element)

* Bennett-Goleman, T., 2001: *Emotional Alchemy* (Crown Publishing, Three Rivers Press)

* Braden, G., 2000: *The Isaiah Effect* (Hay House)

* Byrne, R., 2006: *The Secret* (Simon and Schuster)

The Secret, 2006. Film directed by Drew HERIOT. TS Production LLC

Campbell, D., 1997: *The Mozart Effect* (Quill)

Capra, F., 1975: *The Tao of Physics* (Shambhala Publications Inc.)

Childre, D. and Howard, M., 1999: *The Heartmath Solution* (Harper San Francisco)

* Chopra, D., 1989: *Quantum Healing* (Bantam New Age Books)

* Chopra, D., 1993: *Ageless Body, Timeless Mind* (Rider)

Chopra, D., 1996: *The Seven Spiritual Laws of Success* (Bantam Press)

Cooperrider, D.L. and Srivastva, S., 1987: 'Appreciative Inquiry in Organizational Life'. In W. Pasmore and R. Woodman (eds), *Research in Organizational Change and Development*, vol. 1, pp. 129–169 (JAI Press)

Covey, S., 1992: *The Seven Habits of Highly Effective People* (Simon and Schuster)

* Dossey, L., 1993: *Healing Words* (Harper San Francisco)

Dossey, L., 2002: *Healing Beyond the Body* (Timewarner)

Edwards, G., 1993: *Stepping into the Magic* (Piatkus)

Lazlo, E., 2008: *Quantum Shift in the Global Brain* Inner Traditions (Inner Traditions)

* Emoto, M., 2004: *The Hidden Messages in Water* (Beyond Words)

Frankl, V., 1959: *Man's Search for Meaning* (Beacon Press)

* Gawain, S., 1978: *Creative Visualisation Water* (New World Library. Nataraj)

* Gendlin, E., 1978: *Focusing* (Bantum New Age)

Gilmore, R., 1994: *Alice in Quantumland* (Sigma Press)

Gladwell, M., 2005: *Blink* (Little, Brown)

Goleman, D., 1996: *Emotional Intelligence* (Bloomsbury)

Goleman, D., 2000: *Working with Emotional Intelligence* (Bloomsbury)

Goswami, A., 2004: *The Quantum Doctor* (Hampton Roads)

Goswami, A., 1995: *The Self Aware Universe* (Penguin Putnam Inc.)

* Hawkins, D.R., 1995: *Power versus Force* (Hay House)

Holmes, P. and Karp, M. (eds), 1991: *Psychodrama Inspiration and Technique* (Routledge)

* Keleman, S., 1975: *Your Body Speaks Its Mind* (Center Press)

* Keleman, S., 1985: *Emotional Anatomy* (Center Press)

* Mandell, F., 2003: *Self-Powerment* (Namaste. Dutton)

* McTaggart, L., 2001: *The Field* (Harper Perennial)

Millman, D., 1993: *The Life You Were Born To Live* (H.J. Kramer Inc.)

Myss, C., 1996: *Anatomy of the Spirit* (Reed Business Information)

Myss, C., 2004: *Invisible Acts of Power* (Free Press)

Pert, C., 1997: *Molecules of Emotion* (Touchstone)

* Siegel, B., 1986: *Love, Medicine and Miracles* (Harper)

* Siegel, B., 1989: *Peace, Love and Healing* (Quill)

Talbot, M., 1991: *The Holographic Universe* (HarperCollins)

* Tolle, E., 2001: *The Power of Now* (Namaste. Plume)

Tolle, E., 2003: *Stillness Speaks* (New World Library)

* Tolle, E., 2005: *A New Earth* (Namaste. Plume)

Whitmore, J.K., 2002: *Coaching for Performance* (London. Nicholas Brealey)

Whitworth, L., Kimsey-House, H. and Sandahl, P., 1998: *Co-Active Coaching* (Davies-Black)

Williamson, M., 1994: *A Return to Love* (Harper Spotlight)

* Zohar, D., 1991: *The Quantum Self* (Flamingo)

Index

Please note that page references to footnotes will be followed by the letter, 'n' . Titles of publications beginning with 'A' or 'The' will be filed under the first significant word

abdominal breathing 88–91
Actioned Response 80
advice, quantum skills 40–43
affirmations 123–125
Ageless Body, Timeless Mind
    (Chopra) 18–19, 20
AK (applied kinesiology) 117–120,
    201
Alice in Quantumland (Gilmore) 20
Amour, J. A. 74
amygdala 70
Anatomy of the Spirit (Myss) 106,
    194
ancient Greek/Indian philosophers
    7n
animal metaphors 200–206, 213
applied kinesiology (AK) 117–120,
    201
appreciative enquiry 218–220
Ardell 74
attention
    to emotions 62
    and energy 53–56
    present moment awareness *see*
        present moment awareness
attention-seeking behaviour 134
awareness 62–66, 90
    see also present moment
        awareness
awareness muscle 62–66
    steps to develop 65
    fast and slow feelings 67
    deep breathing 90
    meditation 91
    irritation 98
    feedback, client, behaviour 135,
        212
    smile survey 147
    intuition 175
    psychodrama 227
    present moment 232

back-to-front thinking 195
Bays, Brandon 14, 97
Beck, Aaron T. 29
behaviour, client
    case studies/examples 161–163
    feedback 133–135, 149–150
    impact of 160–165
    power, giving away 197–199
    recognition by client 137
beliefs
    of coach 168–171
    keystone 168, 209–210
Bennett-Goleman, Tara 20
biography 125
biological response mechanism
    66
blame 142
Blink (Gladwell) 148
body language 197–198, 211
body-mind
    case studies/examples
        205–206
    emotions 104
    feelings in body 135, 137, 138,
        156, 192, 207
    present moment awareness
        65–66
    and thoughts 10
brain
    limbic 70–71
    sand analogy 110–111, 216
brainstorming 220
    reverse 222–223
breathing techniques 35, 88–92

cancer 26, 52
Capra, Fritjof 22–23
case studies/examples
    behaviour, client 161–163

case studies/examples *(cont.)*
    emotions 93–95
    focusing technique 107–116
    intuition 176–183
    observations 150–157
    problem solving 221
    psychodrama 226–228
    self-confidence/self-esteem
        199–207
    universal laws 233–236
    words of obligation 139–140
cause and effect, law of 232
CBT (cognitive behaviour therapy)
    29–30, 31, 37
Childre, Doc 73, 74, 105
Chopra, Deepak 20, 91–92, 105
    publications by 18–19, 20,
        230–231
closed questions 180
coaching 4–5
    see also quantum skills
    and entrainment 73
    and feedback 138
    and healing 171
    mindset 35
    outcomes, and coach's beliefs
        168–171
    overall role of coaches 194
    process 14
    and therapy 34–39
    when not to give 164–165
Co-Active Coaching (Whitworth,
    Kimsey-House and Sandahl)
    14
cognitive behaviour therapy (CBT)
    29–30, 31, 37
colours, vibration of 8, 57
communication style 150–154
confidence
    case studies/examples 199–207
    connection to past feelings
        207–208
    inability to remember past
        experiences 211–213
    and power 194–213
    self-knowledge 208
consciousness 22, 23, 40–41, 127,
    169

cosmology, Sankya-Patanjali
    system 7n
Covey, Stephen 154, 227
Creative Visualisation (Gawain) 27
creative visualisation techniques
    see visualisation techniques
crisis, term 216
crystals 8

Damasio, Antonio 71
deep breathing 35, 88–92
Descartes, René 10, 125
detachment, law of 232–233
diabetic disease, and Reiki 25–26
DNA 10, 58
Dossey, Larry 122, 169
Down the Rabbit Hole (film) 20

E+R=O formula 46, 78–85, 88, 90,
    120
    applying 83–85
    and karma 232
    Outcome *see* Outcome
    Response 80
electrons 22
Emotional Anatomy (Keleman)
    106
emotional brain 70
emotional intelligence 67
Emotional Intelligence (Goleman)
    70
emotional pain 16, 18–19, 36, 61,
    63, 64, 190–191
emotions
    awareness 62–65
    case studies/examples 93–94
    and CBT 29
    contagious nature of 72
    definitions 60–61
    fast and slow feelings 66–67
    managing 88–99
    meta-emotion 191
    purpose 61
    and thoughts 60, 81–82
    working with 70–74
Emoto, Masuru 127
empathy 211
energetic footprint 104

energy 104–120
  ancient philosophy 7n
  case studies/examples 107–116
  contra-indications and negative
    scripting 125–126
  and quantum physics 23
  sensations of 64–65
  vibration of 8, 56–57
  in words 122–127, 131–142
energy soup
  E+R=O formula 81
  as field of potentiality 23, 24
  interconnections 46
  and mirror neurons 72
  quantum theory/physics 8,
    56–57
  thoughts 9, 10
energy system, and self-
  description 208
entrainment 73
Event 78, 79
experimenters, intention of 22–23
extraverts/introverts 202–203

faith, leap of 5
family therapy 107
faults, as overuse of a quality 136
feedback
  behaviour, client 133–135,
    149–150
  for benefit of others 132
  about changeable matters 135
  giving immediately following
    occurrence of behaviour 135
  impact of client's behaviour
    160–165
  and intention when giving
    24–25, 137
  method of offering 131–132
  observations 144–157
  on observed behaviour 134
  offering on client's words 138
  permission to offer, asking 134
  reasons for offering 130–131
  rules for giving 132–137
  360 degree 161, 161n, 162,
    186
  and underlying issues 151

feedback *(cont.)*
  violation of rules 149–150
  when not to give 164–165
Feeling Response 80
feeling-being, intuition 156, 157,
  178, 181, 184–187, 190,
  191, 192
feelings
  bland 72, 73
  definition 60–61
  fast and slow 66–67
  feeling in body 138
field of potentiality 23, 24
The Field (McTaggart) 8, 20
fight or flight mechanism 66, 89
first person, talking in 138, 139
focusing
  emotions, managing 92–97
  energy 107–108
  and origins of quantum skills 20
  process of 30
  in visualisation 53
Focusing (Gendlin) 14, 97
Frankl, Viktor 80
frontal cortex, and limbic brain 70

Gawain, Shakti 27
Gendlin, Eugene 14, 20, 97
Gilmore, Robert 20
Gladwell, Malcolm 148
Goleman, Daniel 70
Goswami, Amit 6, 20
gratitude, developing attitude of
  236
gravity 230
GROW model 40, 46
guilt feelings 139

Hawkins, David 118
headache cure 97–98
healing 18–19
  and coaching 171, 178
  present moment awareness 19,
    192
  Reiki 25–27, 31, 105
Healing Words (Dossey) 122, 169
The HeartMath Solution (Childre
  and Martin) 73, 74, 105

Heisenberg, Werner 7n, 23n
The Hidden Messages in Water
    (Emoto) 127
higher mind 110
holographic information 144
holographic theory 105–107, 122,
    144
The Holographic Universe (Talbot)
    105
homeostasis 169
Hopkins, Anthony 149
HPLR (highly task-focused
    individuals) 160
human condition 5, 42, 104, 194,
    228
humanistic psychology 185

integrated healing 105
integration 116–117, 180–181
intention
    of experimenters 22–23
    when giving feedback 24–25, 137
interconnections 46, 50–53
intuition 174–187
    case studies/examples 176–183
    feeling-being 184–187
    irritation 98–99

The Journey (Bays) 14, 97

karma, law of 232
Keleman, Stanley 106
keystone beliefs 168, 209–210
Kimsey-House, Henry 14
kinesiology, applied 117–120, 201

labelling 99, 117, 131, 132,
    134–135, 146, 171, 181,
    217, 221
language
    affirmations 123–125
    body language 197–198, 211
    crisis, term 216
    'hot' words 194
    obligation, words of 139, 140
    use by client 138, 139–142,
        144
    words, holographic theory 122
laughter, inappropriate 145

Law of Attraction 27, 31, 55, 58
    The Secret 230
Law of Gravity 230
leadership 36, 71
The Life You Were Born to Live
    (Millman) 231
limbic brain 70–71
Love, Medicine and Healing
    (Siegel) 122

magnetism 10
Mandela, Nelson 196
Mandell, Faye 14
mannerisms 198
Martin, Howard 73, 74, 105
MBTI (Myers Briggs Type Indicator)
    75
McTaggart, Lynne 8, 20
meditation 90–92
meta-emotion 191
metaphorical journeying 107, 111,
    183, 190
metaphors 190–192
    animal 200–206, 213
    and psychodrama 226
Millman, Dan 231
mind 104–105, 110–111
mirror neurons 71–72
Moreno, Jacob L. 28
muscle-testing 118–120
Myers Briggs Type Indicator (MBTI)
    75
Myss, Caroline 106, 194, 197

natural laws of universe *see*
    universal laws
negative scripting 125–126
neuro linguistic programming
    (NLP) 209
neurons, mirror 71–72
A New Earth (Tolle) 125, 192
NLP (neuro linguistic
    programming) 209

objects, space between as energy
    8
obligation, words of 139–140

observations
    behaviour 134
    case studies/examples 150–157
    describing non-judgmentally
        134–135
    feedback 144–157
Outcome 78, 84
    as new Event 81
    and Response 82–83

particle/wave theory 8, 22
Peace, Love and Healing (Siegel)
    122
personality types 202–203
photons 22, 23, 195
*The Positive Sciences of the Ancient
    Hindus* (Seal) 7n
potentiality, law of 231
power 194–213
    case studies/examples 199–207
    giving away 197–199
    as 'hot' word 194
    personal 194, 198
    of present moment 191–192
Power vs Force (Hawkins) 118
The Power of Now (Tolle) 19, 125,
    192
present moment awareness 18–19,
    30, 232
    body-mind 65–66
    power of present moment
        191–192
    problem solving 216–223
    appreciative enquiry 218–220
    brainstorming 220
    case studies/examples 221
    mindset 216–218
process coaching 14
psychodrama 28, 31
    case studies/examples 226–228
    psychotherapy 107

Quadrant II system 154
quantum skills for coaches
    advice 40–43
    defined 5
    metaphorical journeying 111
    origins 14–31, 230

quantum skills for coaches *(cont.)*
    safety factors 38–39
    quantum field 7
The Quantum Doctor (Goswami) 6,
    20
Quantum Healing (Chopra) 20
quantum leap 5
quantum soup *see* energy soup
quantum theory/physics 20–25
    concepts 6–9
    definition of 'quantum theory'
        5–6
    particle/wave theory 8, 22
    research 30–31
    thoughts, energy of 9–11
The Quantum Self (Zoha) 20

Reiki healing 25–27, 31, 105
Response 78, 80
    contiguous components 80
    and Outcome 82–83
Return to Love (Williamson) 196
revelations, using 208
reverse brainstorming 222–223
risorius (smiling muscle) 148

safety factors, quantum skills
    38–39
sand analogy, brain 110–111, 216
Sandahl, Phil 14
Sankya-Patanjali cosmology
        system 7n
scientific experiments 23, 24
Seal, Brajendranath 7n
second person, talking in 139
The Secret 230
Self Aware Universe (Goswami) 6,
    20
self-coaching 107
self-confidence/self-esteem 195,
    199
self-description, and energy
        system 208
Self-Powerment (Mandell) 14
The Self Aware Universe (Goswami)
    6, 20
The Quantum Doctor (Goswami) 6,
    17

serotonin/serotonin B 73–74
The Seven Habits of Highly Effective People (Covey) 154
The Seven Spiritual Laws of Success (Chopra) 231
'should'/'must' language 139, 140
Siegel, Bernie 122
slow breathing 89
smile survey 147–148
smiling, infrequent 145, 146
spirituality 23, 41, 125, 228, 232
Stein, Gertrude 169
Stillness Speaks (Tolle) 192
stress management 35
struggling 141–142
synchrony, serotonin 74–75

Talbot, Michael 105
The Tao of Physics (Capra) 22
therapy 34–39
    defined 37
Thinking Response 80
thoughts
    cognitive therapy 29
    and emotions 60, 81–82
    quantum theory/physics 9–11
    trains of 110–111
360 degree feedback 161, 161n, 162, 186
time management 154, 227
Tolle, Eckhart 169, 171, 192, 217, 231
    publications by 19, 125, 192
tool kit 15, 34, 40, 41, 46, 50

uncertainty principle 23n
universal laws 230–236
    case studies/examples 233–235
    cause and effect 232
    detachment 232–233
    intention 24–25

universal laws *(cont.)*
    karma 232
    Law of Attraction 27, 31, 55, 58
    potentiality 231
    present moment awareness 232
    and tool kit 41
unknown 169

vibration of energy 8, 56–57
visualisation 27, 31
    attention, and energy 53–56
    cancer patients 52
    detachment, law of 233
    instructions 50–53
    playful approach recommended 55–56
    presenting to client 56–58
    primary rule 55, 61
    unconscious 233

wave detectors 22
'well of pain' experience 15–18, 19, 30, 64
    awareness 53
    and working with emotions 95
wellbeing, feelings of 74
What the Bleep Do We Know? (film) 20, 41
Whitworth, Laura 14
Williamson, Marianne 196
wisdom 25
    of body 62
words, holographic theory 122
worrying 141

yawning 72
yin yang symbol 217

Zoha, Dana 20
zygomatic major (smiling muscle) 148